RADIX LISTENING for the TOEFL iBT®

BLACK LABEL

2

RADIX LISTENING
FOR THE TOEFL iBT® :
BLACK LABEL 2

Series editor	Ji Hyun Kim
Project editors	Yuram Jo, Yeonsue Choi, Hyejin Kim
Contributing writers	Bryce Olk, Nathaniel Galletta, Tamar Harrington, Michael Ledezma, MyAn Le
Design	dots
Editorial designers	In-sun Lee

Photo Credits	www.shutterstock.com

www.neungyule.com

TABLE OF **CONTENTS**

INTRODUCTION

TOEFL®: Test of English as a Foreign Language

The TOEFL is a standardized test developed to assess English language proficiency in an academic setting. By achieving a high score on the TOEFL, you will demonstrate that your skills in English qualify you for admission to a college or university where English is used as the language of instruction. Academic institutions around the world will look at your performance on the TOEFL, so whether you are hoping to study in North America, Australia, Europe, or Asia, this test is the key to your future educational career.

TOEFL Today: TOEFL iBT

The TOEFL Internet-based test (iBT) is the version currently administered in secure testing centers worldwide. It tests reading, listening and writing proficiency, and speaking abilities.

Getting to Know the TOEFL iBT: Important Points

>> The test is divided into four sections: Reading, Listening, Speaking, and Writing. These are the skills that are essential for proficiency in any language.

>> As well as measuring the individual skills listed above, some portions of the test require you to apply various combinations of skills in order to complete a task. Examples of such integrated tasks include:
  - listening to a passage and speaking in response to a question on the passage
  - reading a passage, listening to a second passage, and then speaking in response to a question on the two passages
  - reading a passage, listening to a second passage, and then writing a response to a question on the two passages

>> In each section of the test, a tool bar is displayed on the computer screen. It lists the section and question number you are currently working on, the amount of time remaining, and has help, navigational, and volume buttons. The function buttons may differ slightly from one section to the next.

>> In the Speaking section of the test, you will be required to speak your responses into a microphone. Your input will be digitally recorded and evaluated by ETS's trained scorers.

>> In the Writing section of the test, you will be required to type your responses.

>> There is no section dedicated to grammar, but your grammar skills will be tested indirectly throughout the test, especially in the Speaking and Writing sections.

>> You will be allowed to take notes during all portions of the test, and you will likely find these notes very helpful when answering the questions.

>> You can view your scores in your ETS account approximately 6 days after your test date. You'll receive an email when your scores are available, and you can access your account online or via the official TOEFL® app.

Getting to Know the TOEFL iBT: Test Format

You will take all four sections of the test (Reading, Listening, Speaking, and Writing) on the same day. The duration of the entire test is about four hours.

Test Section	Description of Tasks	Timing
Reading	3–4 passages, each approximately 700 words 10 questions on each passage	54–72 minutes
Listening	3-4 lectures, each 3-5 minutes long 6 questions per lecture 2–3 conversations, each around 3 minutes long 5 questions per conversation	41–57 minutes
BREAK		10 minutes
Speaking	4 tasks • 1 independent task – speak about personal knowledge and experience • 3 integrated tasks – read-listen-speak / listen-speak	17 minutes
Writing	2 tasks • 1 independent task – write about personal knowledge and experience • 1 integrated task – read-listen-write	50 minutes

Score Scales

You will receive a score between 0 and 30 for each section of the test. Your total score is the sum of these four scores and will be between 0 and 120.

Registering for the TOEFL iBT

The most convenient way to register to take the TOEFL iBT is online by visiting the "Register for the TOEFL® Test" section of the TOEFL website (www.ets.org/toefl). Here, you can check current listings of testing centers and schedules. It is also possible to register for the test by phone and by mail. For more information, consult the TOEFL iBT Bulletin, which can be downloaded or ordered from the TOEFL website. It is free and features important information regarding the registration process.

GUIDE TO LISTENING

For students pursuing studies in English-speaking environments, listening comprehension is an essential skill, as information will be delivered through lectures and conversations. The Listening section of the TOEFL iBT will require you to demonstrate your understanding of English as it is spoken in academic settings in North America and throughout the world. Questions in the Listening section are designed to test:

1. Your basic comprehension of a lecture or conversation, including the main idea and key details
2. Your understanding of the speaker's purpose for relating certain information and his or her attitude about this information
3. Your ability to synthesize information from various parts of a lecture or conversation in order to understand its organization and the relationships between its ideas, and to draw inferences based on it

Listening Section Content

The material you will hear in the Listening section will include academic lectures typical of a classroom setting and conversations related to student life. The speech will accurately reflect real-life spoken English, and may include the following features: polite interruptions, mistakes and corrections, hesitations and repetitions. Although many of the speakers in the Listening section will have standard American accents, some may have a regional U.S. accent or an accent from another English-speaking country.

Academic Lectures

There are two formats of academic lectures that appear in the Listening section: monologues and interactive lectures. In a monologue, the professor is the only one who speaks. In an interactive lecture, one or two students will participate in a discussion with the professor about the information he or she is presenting. The subject matter of both monologues and interactive lectures imitates what is commonly covered in introductory-level classes at colleges and universities. Lecture topics are quite varied, but no prior knowledge or expertise is required to understand the material. You will be able to answer all the questions using only the information contained in the lectures.

Conversations

Unlike the lectures, the conversations in the TOEFL iBT do not involve specific academic material. Instead, they are concerned with problems and situations typical of student life. One speaker is usually a student, and the other can be a professor, teaching assistant, office clerk, librarian, another student, etc.

Types of Questions

The questions found in the Listening section can be divided into seven categories.

Question Type	Testing Point
Main Idea	The overall content or purpose of the lecture or conversation
Detail	Important details introduced in the lecture or conversation
Function	The speaker's reason for making a specific statement in the lecture or conversation
Attitude	The speaker's attitude toward or degree of certainty about ideas in the lecture or conversation
Organization	The overall relationship between major ideas in the lecture
Connecting Content	Relationships that have been stated or clearly implied in the lecture or conversation
Inference	The speaker's intended meaning or implication in the lecture or conversation

Important Points to Keep in Mind

» You can take notes on all of the listening materials as you hear them. This is recommended, as you are not expected to memorize the material you hear.

» There will be a picture or pictures shown on the computer screen to provide context for each lecture or conversation.

» For lectures that use specialized terms, the new vocabulary may appear on a "blackboard screen" on the computer. This imitates the way a professor might write important terms on a blackboard. The purpose of these screens is to assist in your understanding of the lecture, but they do not necessarily present information related to the questions you will have to answer.

» When you see a headphone icon next to a question, it means you will have to listen again to an excerpt from the lecture or conversation before answering the question.

» There is no time limit for individual questions in the Listening section, but you must budget your time in order to finish the entire section within the allotted 60–90 minutes.

» A tool bar is displayed on the computer screen. It lists the section and question number you are currently working on, the amount of time remaining, and has help, navigational, and volume buttons.
Keep in mind that in the Listening section, you cannot return to a question after you have confirmed your answer.

Tactics for the TOEFL iBT Listening Section

To strengthen your listening skills before taking the TOEFL iBT, it is essential to frequently expose yourself to sources of spoken English. Watching movies and television and listening to radio programs on various topics are simple and effective ways of doing this. To receive practice specifically with academic speech, check out the audio material available at libraries and bookstores. You may find it helpful to obtain a transcript of the material so you can read along as you listen.

During the test, remember to:

- make a note of new words and concepts that are presented in the lectures
- remain focused by thinking about what the speakers will likely say next
- consider each speaker's motivation and why they present certain information
- concentrate on the organization of the lecture or conversation so you can notice the difference between changes in topic and digressions
- listen for key words that demonstrate how important ideas are related to each other

HOW TO USE THIS BOOK

This book gives you instruction, practice, and strategies for performing well on the TOEFL iBT Listening Section. It will familiarize you with the appearance and format of the TOEFL iBT and help you prepare for the TOEFL test efficiently.

Each unit in the book corresponds to one of the seven question types in the Listening Section. Each unit consists of the following:
- An **Introduction** that provides basic information about the question type
- **Basic Drills** that offer short listening materials to give examples of the question type being covered and allow you to become familiar with it
- **Listening Practice** involving longer listening materials that will improve essential skills
- **iBT Practice** that provides extensive exercises
- **Note-Takings** that help you practice and improve note-taking skills for the TOEFL iBT
- **Dictations** that require a focus on accuracy, general comprehension, and special features of pronunciation while you transcribe or orally reproduce what you hear
- A **Vocabulary Review** that offers a variety of activities designed to help you review and master essential vocabulary

In addition, this book contains three **Actual Practice Tests** to help you measure your progress, and these appear after unit 7.

PART

A

Basic
Comprehension
Questions

01 Main Idea

Introduction

- Main Idea questions focus on testing overall understanding of a conversation or lecture.
- These questions ask about the topic of the conversation or lecture.
- A Main Idea question is given for every conversation or lecture, and it will always appear as the first question for the passage.

Question Types

1. Question forms for conversations:
   - Why does the student go to see the professor?
   - What problem does the student have?
   - What are the speakers mainly discussing?

2. Question forms for lectures:
   - What is the lecture mainly about?
   - What is the main point of the lecture?
   - What aspect of X does the professor mainly discuss?

Strategy

1. Listen closely to the start of the conversation or lecture.
   (1) Conversations: The main idea commonly concerns the student's problem. Identify the problem by focusing on the start of the conversation.
   (2) Lectures: The professor introduces the subject of his/her talk at the start of the lecture.

2. You must have a complete understanding of the content. While listening, focus on the overall flow of the passage while noting the major points. An effective approach is to write down key words and phrases.

3. The solution to the Main Idea questions can be found in key words or phrases in the passage that have been paraphrased. Therefore, answer choices containing exact words and phrases from the passage are probably not correct.

Basic Drills

1 What is the lecture mainly about?

   Ⓐ The cooperative hunting of wolves

   Ⓑ The social structure of wolf packs

   Ⓒ Wolves' responsibility for their families

   Ⓓ The hierarchical similarity between wolves and birds

2 What is the lecture mainly about?

   Ⓐ The structure of the Earth's crust

   Ⓑ What makes an earthquake happen

   Ⓒ Locations of frequent earthquakes

   Ⓓ How plate tectonics is used to predict earthquakes

3 What is the lecture mainly about?

   Ⓐ an anthropologist's early studies related to social distancing

   Ⓑ how social distancing is different from proxemics

   Ⓒ the anthropologist who rediscovered social distancing

   Ⓓ why social distancing is no longer effective

Dictation

Listen and fill in the blanks.

1. Anyway, it has long been established that _____
   _____ .

2. At the top of any wolf hierarchy are the senior… or alpha males, presiding over the pack and
   _____ .

3. The alpha male's immediate subordinates are the other mature wolves, _____
   _____ .

4. Immature wolves then follow, and they will not be _____
   _____ .

5. So, _____
   around the 1960s with the development of the theory of plate tectonics.

6. Imagine cracking a hard-boiled egg so that _____
   _____ .

7. The… uhm… _____ on the plate
   boundaries and eventually becomes so great that the plates er… the plates _____
   _____ , releasing energy that has been built up
   for hundreds or thousands of years.

8. The colliding plates can cause so much energy to be released that _____
   _____ .

9. It _____ in the writings of Edward T.
   Hall.

10. Hall _____ ,
    especially in how they established and defined their public and personal spaces.

11. He did, however, _____
    the spaces between one another.

12. He believed it _____ and behaviors
    associated with Americans.

● Listening Practice 01

OFFICE HOURS

1 What do the student and the professor mainly discuss?

(A) The student's essay about a story

(B) The elements of story writing

(C) The student's outline for an essay

(D) The first draft of the student's story

2 What is the student going to do to improve his work?

Click on 3 answers.

(A) Reorganize the plot

(B) Take out unnecessary words

(C) Insert interjections in the dialog

(D) Create a new character

(E) Remove direct explanations of characters

Listen again to part of the conversation. Then answer the question.

3 Why does the professor say this: 🎧

(A) To encourage the student before he rewrites the story

(B) To persuade the student to become a writer

(C) To show the student that he has potential in writing

(D) To emphasize the importance of collaborating with other writers

Listen and fill in the blanks.

Student: *[knocking]* Are you busy right now?

Professor: No, not at all. Come on in.

S: I was wondering _____ .

P: Yes, I did. You've got some great ideas. You presented a _____

_____ .

S: Thanks. Do you have any suggestions?

P: Oh yes... yes. This is a good first draft, _____ .

S: Okay... what exactly were the problems _____ ?

P: Well, take the conversation between Ned and Rebecca. It doesn't really seem like a conversation at all, does it? Let me see... Okay, here... Ned just goes on and on and Rebecca doesn't say a word. In real life, Rebecca _____ into the conversation, don't you think?

S: Yeah, I see what you mean. Actually _____

_____ of Ned. That's why I... well anyway... I can work in a few interjections.

P: Good. Secondly, a well-written story lets the reader make their own observations about characters. _____ what each character is like.

S: I thought you said characterization was one of the most important things.

P: It is... but _____ . Let your characters' personalities make themselves known through their behavior. You need to respect your readers...

_____ .

S: Okay. I misunderstood the notion of characterization...

P: One more thing. _____ . Look here, you said that Ned was yelling loudly. *[laughing]* Have you ever heard anyone yell softly? By definition, yelling is loud. Then you've got Rebecca pointing to the "long-necked giraffe" at the zoo. All giraffes have long necks. So, you don't need to use those unnecessary adjectives and adverbs, which sort of umm... _____ .

S: Yes, you're right. *[discouraged]* Hmm... I guess I have a lot of work to do.

P: Well... as a writer, most of the work that you do will be in revising. _____

_____ . I look forward to your second draft.

S: Thanks for the advice.

P: That's what I'm here for.

Listening Practice 02

HISTORY

---

1   What is the lecture mainly about?

  Ⓐ The factors that brought about the Black Death

  Ⓑ Medical procedures used during the Black Death

  Ⓒ The Black Death's positive impact on the medical field

  Ⓓ The popularity of medical books during the Black Death

2   What can be inferred about medicine before the Black Death?

  Ⓐ Physicians knew medicine had to advance further to find cures for diseases.

  Ⓑ Religious beliefs hindered medical study from developing.

  Ⓒ Ancient Greek medical texts were rarely used by physicians.

  Ⓓ New scientific theories were being presented by many doctors.

3   According to the professor, what changes took place after the Black Death?

Click on 2 answers.

  Ⓐ Medical books were published in English for ordinary people.

  Ⓑ Many medical institutions were built across Europe.

  Ⓒ Doctors started to experiment with real human bodies.

  Ⓓ A cure was discovered for the Black Plague.

Listen and fill in the blanks.

Professor: All right. So the Plague, or Black Death, _____
_____ during the 13th and 14th centuries.
_____.
However, this tragedy resulted in some good. One of the most immediate benefits was
reform of the medical profession.
First... umm... medieval medicine _____
in combating the Black Death, but the consequences of its ineptitude _____
_____. Both, uh... both physicians and scientists
alike _____ in order to fight disease
and enhance understanding of human physiology. Back then, medical learning was based
on the texts of the Ancient Greek physicians Hippocrates and Galen... written in Latin. In the
wake of the Plague, the uh... _____
_____, which were based on animal autopsies and
were over a thousand years old, and _____.
Arguably the most significant breakthrough was the introduction of research based around the
dissection of human cadavers. _____
_____, as it believed that a soul would never
reach heaven if the body were dismembered. However, _____,
and by 1380, physicians' knowledge of anatomy was fairly accurate. This new focus on
scientific theories and analyses _____.
Uhm... in addition, the appearance of medical books written in everyday language is worth
discussing.
Student: You mean they were written in everyday English?
P: Absolutely! As I told you just before, at that time most medical books were written in Latin.
S: So _____?
P: As you can guess, many doctors... umm... including university professors _____
_____ because they felt at
risk from the disease. Such a chronic lack of trained physicians caused ordinary people to
acquire medical guides and take command of their own health. But with... uh... high rates
of illiteracy in Latin _____
_____. Thus, medical books began to be
published in English, providing them with more accessible medical knowledge.

Listening Practice 03

SPORTS

1 What is the lecture mainly about?

ⓐ How to successfully coach a soccer team

ⓑ The various responsibilities of a sports coach

ⓒ Similarities between sports management and business management

ⓓ The results of a survey about coaching athletes

2 According to the professor, what duties must coaches perform?

Click on 3 answers.

ⓐ Organizing fundraising events

ⓑ Making hotel reservations

ⓒ Providing motivation for athletes

ⓓ Tending to athletes' injuries

ⓔ Managing a team's finances

Listen again to part of the lecture. Then answer the question.

3 Why does the professor say this: 🎧

ⓐ To apologize for being unable to help the student

ⓑ To apply his lecture to the student's situation

ⓒ To recognize that his suggestion is impractical

ⓓ To suggest that the student change his work schedule

Listen and fill in the blanks.

Professor: Now, class, whenever we talk about a sports team or individual athlete, um... _____. That is, they all have a coach. And, uh, it's easy to maintain that the coach is the most important person to that team or athlete. Do you agree with that?

Student 1: I don't know, professor. I mean, _____ _____ to determine whether a team wins or loses. Sure, the coach can implement some strategies and _____ _____, but...

P: Hold on there. I think _____ most people have about coaches. You see, coaches have to do _____ _____athletes about their sport. Much more. Besides instructing athletes, successful coaches have to be able to demonstrate the skills they're teaching. _____... um, handling players' emotions and keeping the enthusiasm level high. And actually, there was a recent survey showing that the majority of coaches feel one of the most trying parts of their job is, uh, _____.

S1: You're saying that coaches have administrative duties?

P: You bet. Administrative duties are paramount. They have to _____ _____ ... um, they have to find appropriate competitions for their teams to participate in. And _____.

Student 2: Professor? _____, but... I've volunteered to work at Dawson Elementary as a coach this summer.

P: That's great! What sport are you coaching?

S2: Soccer. And, well... I've played soccer before, but I've never coached it. Do you have any advice for me?

P: Sure. I was just talking about the administrative duties of a coach. Most students who want to become coaches take sports management courses here at the university. But _____ _____. That'll really help you understand the administrative aspects of coaching. Oh, wait... you said you're coaching this summer, so... _____. But bear that in mind for the future.

S2: Okay, I will. Thanks.

● iBT Practice 01

TOEFL Listening

VOLUME   HELP   OK   NEXT

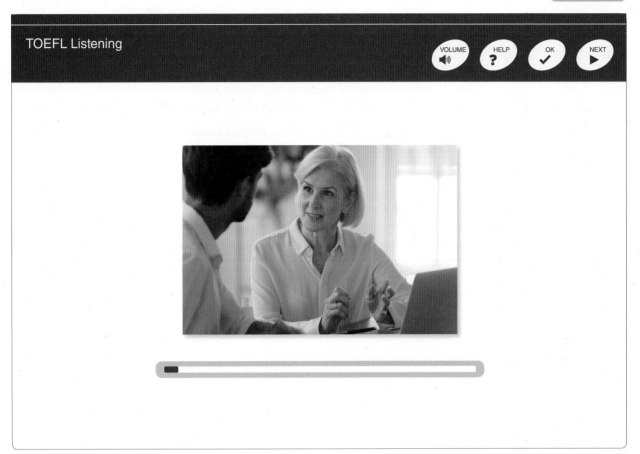

Note-Taking

1. What does the professor mainly discuss with the student?
   - (A) How the student can improve his paper
   - (B) The student's low participation in the class
   - (C) The difference between Renaissance art and Baroque art
   - (D) The importance of human emotions in discussing art

2. Which of the following does the student feel most comfortable with?
   - (A) Discussing objective points
   - (B) Sharing subjective opinions
   - (C) Drawing a neat conclusion
   - (D) Expressing emotions through art

3. Why does the professor explain her grading policy?
   - (A) To explain why the student needs to rewrite his paper
   - (B) To demonstrate the importance of handing in papers on time
   - (C) To emphasize that lack of participation will affect the student's grade
   - (D) To persuade the student to do extra work to pass the class

4. Why does the professor ask the student the difference between Renaissance art and Baroque art?
   - (A) To test the student's knowledge of art history
   - (B) To stress the importance of knowing it
   - (C) To motivate the student to present his thoughts in class
   - (D) To suggest the student do a presentation on it

Listen again to part of the conversation. Then answer the question.

5. What does the professor imply when she says this: 🎧
   - (A) She thinks the student cheated on the paper.
   - (B) She thinks the student did a better job than she had expected.
   - (C) She doesn't think the paper was well written.
   - (D) She expects more from the student in the future.

iBT Practice 02

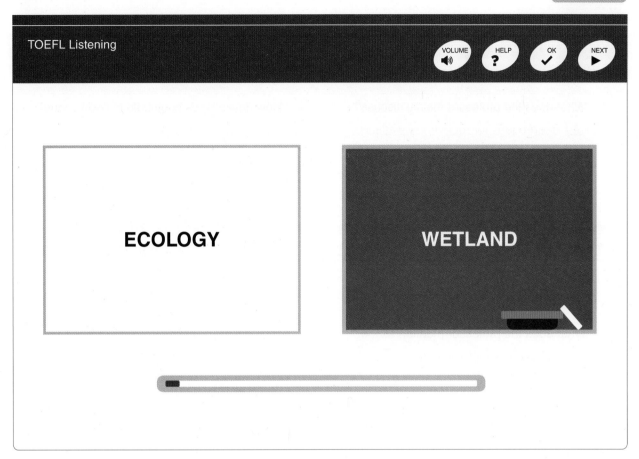

TOEFL Listening

VOLUME   HELP   OK   NEXT

ECOLOGY

WETLAND

Note-Taking

1. What does the professor mainly discuss?
   (A) Techniques for recovering wetlands
   (B) The economic potential of wetlands
   (C) Wildlife that inhabits wetlands
   (D) The beneficial roles of wetlands

2. What does the professor mention as the reason for wetlands' biodiversity?
   Click on 2 answers.
   (A) Wetlands offer easy accessibility.
   (B) Wetlands provide an abundant food supply.
   (C) Wetlands offer safe shelter.
   (D) Wetlands supply a quality water source.

3. Why does the professor mention kidneys?
   (A) To provide background information and ask a question
   (B) To explain their function and encourage the students to answer
   (C) To clarify the concept and introduce the main point
   (D) To use the analogy and help the students' understanding

4. How do wetlands contribute to flood control?
   Click on 2 answers.
   (A) Wetlands reduce flooding by storing water.
   (B) Wetlands purify surface water nutrients and sediments.
   (C) Wetland animals build waterways and adjust the flow of water.
   (D) Wetland plants protect shorelines from erosion.

5. What is the professor's attitude toward the future of wetlands?
   (A) He thinks wetlands are in too much danger to try anything.
   (B) He is cautiously optimistic that things are improving.
   (C) He suggests we should create artificial replacements for wetlands.
   (D) He shows great confidence in the success of restoring wetlands.

Listen again to part of the lecture.
Then answer the question.

6. What does the professor imply about wetlands?
   (A) The economic value of wetlands has increased.
   (B) Wetlands made residential development difficult.
   (C) Wetlands were undervalued in the past.
   (D) The use of wetlands has been changed.

VOLUME HELP OK NEXT

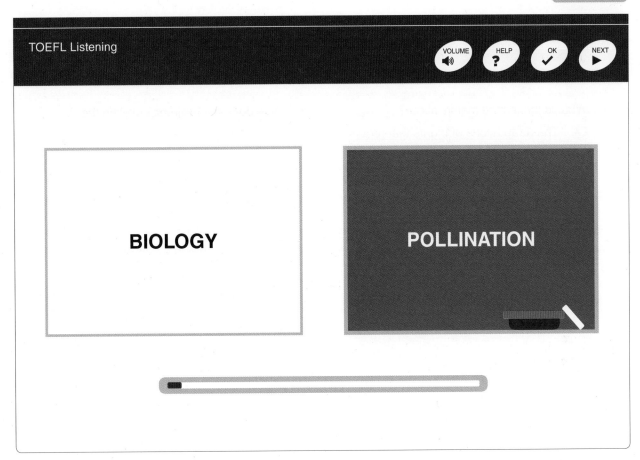

BIOLOGY

POLLINATION

PART A

UNIT 01 MAIN IDEA

Note-Taking

1. What is the lecture mainly about?
   - (A) The adaptations of plants that require pollinators
   - (B) The relationship between seed plants and pollinators
   - (C) The reproductive processes of seed plants
   - (D) The similarities between four pollination methods

2. What happens during the process of self-pollination?
   - (A) The use of a pollinator enables pollen from a single plant to reach the stigma.
   - (B) The male and female reproductive structures of a single plant come in contact.
   - (C) Pollen travels from one plant to another using wind, birds, or bats.
   - (D) Fertilization occurs as a result of different species exchanging pollen.

3. What represents the difference between self-pollination and self-pollenization?
   - (A) Whether it occurs all year-round
   - (B) Whether it is affected by weather
   - (C) Whether pollen spreads to the same plant
   - (D) Whether it needs a pollinator

4. How does the professor explain the difference between plants according to pollinators?
   - (A) By comparing the features of plants
   - (B) By explaining plants' scientific classifications
   - (C) By describing the kinds of pollinators
   - (D) By contrasting the process of pollination

5. What does the professor say about plants that are pollinated by wind?
   - (A) They rely on self-pollenization more than cross-pollination.
   - (B) They have large petals compared to plants that use biological pollinators.
   - (C) They have large stigmas to gather passing pollen grains.
   - (D) They have stronger scents than plants that rely on other pollinators.

Listen again to part of the lecture.
Then answer the question.

6. Why does the professor say this:
   - (A) To correct the students' misunderstanding about an idea
   - (B) To acknowledge that a concept in the lecture is difficult
   - (C) To shift the point of the lecture
   - (D) To emphasize an important point

Vocabulary Check

- [ ] establish
- [ ] hierarchically
- [ ] hierarchy
- [ ] pack
- [ ] pecking order
- [ ] alpha
- [ ] preside
- [ ] dominance
- [ ] privilege
- [ ] distinct
- [ ] subordinate
- [ ] outcast
- [ ] take precedence over

- [ ] take off
- [ ] plate tectonics
- [ ] slab
- [ ] crack
- [ ] hard-boiled
- [ ] molten
- [ ] lava
- [ ] sporadically
- [ ] stress
- [ ] collide

- [ ] anthropologist
- [ ] coin
- [ ] proxemics
- [ ] specifically
- [ ] fundamental
- [ ] psyche
- [ ] trait
- [ ] hold true
- [ ] coronavirus
- [ ] pandemic

- [ ] measure
- [ ] readily

- [ ] draft
- [ ] interject
- [ ] interjection
- [ ] characterization
- [ ] notion
- [ ] redundancy
- [ ] by definition
- [ ] tension
- [ ] revise

- [ ] the Plague
- [ ] epidemic
- [ ] catastrophic
- [ ] ineptitude
- [ ] physiology
- [ ] in the wake of
- [ ] shortcoming
- [ ] autopsy
- [ ] arguably
- [ ] breakthrough
- [ ] dissection
- [ ] cadaver
- [ ] mutilation
- [ ] dismember
- [ ] anatomy
- [ ] flee
- [ ] chronic
- [ ] illiteracy

- [ ] implement
- [ ] impart
- [ ] pinpoint
- [ ] misconception

- [ ] motivator
- [ ] trying
- [ ] organizational
- [ ] administrative
- [ ] paramount
- [ ] lodging
- [ ] budget

- [ ] keen
- [ ] insight
- [ ] commit
- [ ] objectivity
- [ ] objective
- [ ] be out of one's element
- [ ] subjective
- [ ] applaud
- [ ] have the guts to-v
- [ ] superb
- [ ] count
- [ ] sensitivity
- [ ] symmetrical
- [ ] all over the place

- [ ] wetland
- [ ] periodically
- [ ] submerge
- [ ] marsh
- [ ] bog
- [ ] estuary
- [ ] convert
- [ ] impede
- [ ] residential
- [ ] reside
- [ ] expendable
- [ ] biodiversity

- [ ] detritus
- [ ] in excess of
- [ ] notable
- [ ] sediment
- [ ] kidney
- [ ] runoff
- [ ] pollutant
- [ ] uptake
- [ ] shoreline
- [ ] erosion
- [ ] stabilize
- [ ] accumulation

- [ ] pollination
- [ ] seed plant
- [ ] pollen grain
- [ ] stamen
- [ ] ovule
- [ ] carpel
- [ ] stigma
- [ ] fertilize
- [ ] fertilization
- [ ] pollinator
- [ ] dull
- [ ] deposit
- [ ] petal
- [ ] flashy

Vocabulary Review

A **Choose the correct word for each definition.**

| flashy   motivator   chronic   periodically   budget   misconception |

1. an erroneous belief: _____
2. the money allocated for a particular purpose: _____
3. at regular intervals: _____
4. looking big or bright, and intended to get attention: _____
5. an agent that causes one to act: _____

B **Choose the best word or phrase to explain the underlined word.**

1. If you are <u>dismembered</u>, you lose a _____.
   - (A) bet
   - (B) membership
   - (C) body part
   - (D) sporting event

2. If you <u>coin</u> a word or a phrase, you are the first person to _____ it.
   - (A) remember
   - (B) invent
   - (C) blame
   - (D) notice

3. If you <u>flee</u> a person or thing, you _____ them.
   - (A) go after
   - (B) rely on
   - (C) fall behind
   - (D) escape from

4. If something is <u>expendable</u>, you _____ it.
   - (A) can't afford
   - (B) can expand
   - (C) don't need
   - (D) don't believe

C **Choose the best word to complete each sentence.**

1. His tendency to avoid responsibility is one of his many _____.
   - (A) insights
   - (B) shortcomings
   - (C) redundancies
   - (D) synonyms

2. The waves crashing against the cliffs are causing _____.
   - (A) uptake
   - (B) erosion
   - (C) runoff
   - (D) dissection

3. Heavy rain is _____ the progress of rescue workers.
   - (A) committing
   - (B) revising
   - (C) converting
   - (D) impeding

4. A caricature is a(n) _____ presentation of a person or action in a humorous and critical way.
   - (A) notable
   - (B) outcast
   - (C) distorted
   - (D) molten

D Choose the correct word to complete each sentence.

1. My family takes precedence _____ my job. (with / over)
2. The business really _____ off when people started talking about the new product. (made / took)
3. In the _____ of the earthquake, the whole city lay in ruin. (wake / tension)
4. Your essay is all _____ the place. You need to stick to a topic. (over / about)
5. We are creating in _____ of one million tons of trash per year. (disposal / excess)

E Choose the word or phrase that is closest in meaning to the underlined word.

1. Humility is an admirable trait.
   - (A) quality
   - (B) humanity
   - (C) pursuit
   - (D) target

2. We're going to first pinpoint the problems and then brainstorm possible solutions.
   - (A) create
   - (B) stabilize
   - (C) identify
   - (D) solve

3. We all applaud you for your diligence in seeing this project through to the end.
   - (A) laugh at
   - (B) look back on
   - (C) chastise
   - (D) praise

4. Squid deposit their eggs on the seafloor.
   - (A) place
   - (B) arrange
   - (C) hatch
   - (D) clean

5. These are trying times for the family and we should show our support.
   - (A) administrative
   - (B) valuable
   - (C) adventurous
   - (D) difficult

F Choose the word that is the opposite of the underlined word.

1. The newspaper, or more specifically, the editor, was taken to court for publishing the photographs.
   - (A) directly
   - (B) accurately
   - (C) generally
   - (D) reliably

2. The Constitution ensures our fundamental rights.
   - (A) ethical
   - (B) inessential
   - (C) proven
   - (D) economical

3. The hurricane was catastrophic for the region.
   - (A) sporadic
   - (B) distinct
   - (C) paramount
   - (D) beneficial

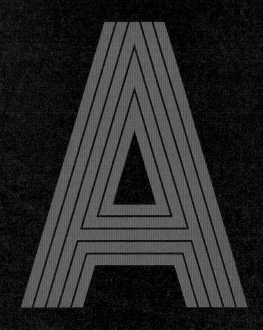

PART A

Basic Comprehension Questions

Introduction

- Detail questions test understanding of key details mentioned in the conversation or lecture.
- Sometimes, these questions ask whether a piece of given information is true or false.
- Occasionally, these questions require 2-3 correct answers.
- 2 or more questions are given for each passage.

Question Types

1. Question forms that require one correct answer:
   - According to the professor, what is the problem with the X method?
   - Which of the following is NOT mentioned as X?

2. Question forms that require two or more correct answers:
   - What are the key features of X mentioned in the lecture? Click on 2 answers.
   - According to the professor, what are the reasons for X? Click on 3 answers.

Strategy

1. Identify the topic of the conversation or lecture immediately. Then take notes, concentrating on information related to the main topic.
   (1) Conversations: The content commonly concerns possible solutions for a student's problem or dilemma. When listening, focus on the solutions being suggested.
   (2) Lectures: Questions concern information directly related to the main topic and not to less important details. Definitions, examples, reasons, results, features, etc. are used to support the main idea.

2. In the majority of cases, answer choices that contain the exact words or expressions given in the conversation or lecture are incorrect. Generally, correct answer choices present information from the conversation or lecture in a paraphrased form.

● Basic Drills

1   Which of the following is NOT mentioned as behavior of a male parakeet during courtship?

Ⓐ Singing for the female

Ⓑ Touching the female's bill with his

Ⓒ Changing his eye color

Ⓓ Puffing his feathers up

2   Why are O'Keeffe's paintings called semi-abstract?

Ⓐ Because she depicts familiar things in an unrealistic way

Ⓑ Because she describes objects in full detail

Ⓒ Because she puts more emphasis on color than form

Ⓓ Because she mixes many colors to express idealized images

3   What is NOT mentioned as a feature of black ice?

Ⓐ It is see-through.

Ⓑ It often forms on bridges.

Ⓒ It can cause traffic accidents.

Ⓓ It occurs during heavy snow.

Dictation

Listen and fill in the blanks.

1. Courtship behavior, or courtship display, _____
   _____ .

2. It is _____ .

3. The sequence and... erm... the variety of courtship behaviors vary widely among species, but
   _____ .

4. _____ by going through his
   courtship display to the female.

5. He repeats this routine several times, each time _____
   _____ .

6. I mean... she was meticulous and steadfast _____
   _____ .

7. I mean while her paintings often depict recognizable images and objects... umm... including
   such mundane subjects as flowers, rocks, shells, animal bones... _____
   _____ .

8. Through her paintings, she reduces her subjects _____
   _____ .

9. The boundaries of her simplification of real-life objects stretch beyond convention, and
   _____ .

10. _____
    is a phenomenon called black ice.

11. It's actually transparent, _____
    _____ .

12. To make matters worse, _____
    _____ on bridges and overpasses.

13. As their tires begin to lose traction, they slam on their brakes, losing control of their vehicles
    and, _____
    _____ .

● Listening Practice 01

> **OFFICE HOURS**

1 Why does the student go to see his professor?

   Ⓐ To decide on a topic for his presentation

   Ⓑ To have his presentation date changed

   Ⓒ To invite the professor to a photo awards ceremony

   Ⓓ To ask the professor to write a review of his father's book

2 What is true about the student's father?

   Ⓐ He published a book with essays and photos.

   Ⓑ He will receive an award for photography.

   Ⓒ He majored in French literature.

   Ⓓ He is familiar with the student's professor.

3 What is the professor's attitude toward the book the student's father published?

   Ⓐ She is relieved it was finally published.

   Ⓑ She is unsure of its success.

   Ⓒ She has an interest in it.

   Ⓓ She shows indifference toward it.

Dictation 01

Listen and fill in the blanks.

Student: Excuse me, Dr. Reynolds, _____?

Professor: Sure, what is it?

S: Well, _____.

P: Hmm... Why do you need to do that? _____
_____ I want you to do it as scheduled.

S: I know... I'd like to present it as scheduled as well. But today I got news that my father is receiving an award on the same day _____. It would mean a lot to him _____. All of my family is supposed to be there.

P: Okay. _____?

S: Next Friday.

P: Hmm... *[suspicious]* Do you want to do your presentation _____
_____?

S: It doesn't matter to me. _____.

P: Oh, okay. *[relieved]* I'll see what the others in the class think. I'm sure _____
_____.
If you wanted to go later, that might be a different story, but if you're prepared to go earlier, it should be fine.

S: Great. I appreciate that.

P: What does your father do, anyway?

S: He's a photographer.

P: Oh, _____?

S: No, it's actually for a book. He _____
French novelists and their works and he included photos of them.

P: Oh, so your father is interested in literature too. What's his name?

S: Jason Tompkinson.

P: *[surprisingly]* Ah... really? _____...
and I've heard about that book but I didn't realize Jason Tompkinson was behind it. Wow... what a unique idea. I love French literature. _____
_____.

S: Oh, really? It's great to hear that. I think I can get you one. I'm sure my father would love to give a copy of his book to you.

P: That sounds great! *[pleasantly]* I didn't know I had the son of Jason Tompkinson in my class.

● Listening Practice 02

ENTOMOLOGY

TERMITES

1   What does the professor mainly discuss?

   Ⓐ How termites adapt their environment to fit their needs

   Ⓑ The various methods termites use to search for food

   Ⓒ How termites are more social than other insects

   Ⓓ A technique used by termites to expand their colonies

2   Which of the following is NOT mentioned about termites?

   Ⓐ They are social insects with a hierarchical system.

   Ⓑ They have sensitive and weak bodies.

   Ⓒ Most of them do not fully mature.

   Ⓓ They actively search for food at night.

3   What does the professor say about termites' nests?

Click on 2 answers.

   Ⓐ They are built of a mixture of wood and leaves.

   Ⓑ They are located in moist soil.

   Ⓒ They constantly retain heat.

   Ⓓ They are vulnerable to enemy attack.

Listen and fill in the blanks.

Professor: Now, let's take a look at another type of social insect. The subterranean termite _____ with populations that can number in the, um... in the millions. Like other social insects, they _____ workers, warriors, and breeders. Biologically speaking, _____ _____. With the exception of breeding males and females, most termites are _____... they are deaf and blind, and their bodies are soft and fragile, _____ _____ to their environment.

Student: Excuse me, Professor. I'm just wondering... if termites are so delicate, how do they survive so well? I mean... _____.

P: Oh, that's just what I want to talk about today: how termites control their environment for survival. Well, as I said, termites are a fragile creature. _____ _____. They require a warm environment, as _____ _____. When surface temperatures are unsuitable, they migrate deeper into the soil. And because _____ _____, termites require a ready supply of water to keep themselves hydrated. To achieve this, subterranean termites build their colonies in moist soil. For example, they are _____ _____. This is not all. Around their nest, termites build a hard wall made of soil, saliva and other bodily secretions, which not only protects the nest from predators, _____ _____. So, when the outside environment is unwelcoming, termites survive by controlling their nest. It's pretty impressive! And when termites forage above ground, they have an even more, uh, _____ _____. If they find themselves needing to cross a dry, unwelcoming climate, _____ _____. These tubes, usually a fourth to one inch wide, serve as warm, dark, humid highways... the perfect conditions for a foraging termite.

● Listening Practice 03

GEOLOGY

1   What is the lecture mainly about?

     Ⓐ   The conditions involved in the formation of diamonds

     Ⓑ   How the quality and value of a diamond is determined

     Ⓒ   The physical characteristics of natural diamonds

     Ⓓ   How volcanic eruptions can produce diamonds

2   Which of the following is mentioned as a condition for creating diamonds?

Click on 2 answers.

     Ⓐ   High pressure

     Ⓑ   High energy waves

     Ⓒ   High temperature

     Ⓓ   High moisture levels

3   What does the professor say about kimberlite?

     Ⓐ   It is a stable region that contains many diamonds.

     Ⓑ   It is a rock that draws diamonds toward the earth's surface.

     Ⓒ   It is a place where microdiamonds are formed.

     Ⓓ   It is a geological impact caused by a meteorite.

Listen and fill in the blanks.

Professor: _____ in the world is also

one of the most valuable... and is considered by many to be one of the most beautiful. I'm

talking, of course, about diamonds.

Now, one of the reasons why _____

_____. And the reason they are so rare is

that the conditions required to create a diamond are not only extreme, they are also quite

specific, _____. Some sort of material containing

carbon must be, um, _____,

and this must take place in a low temperature environment. And please keep in mind,

when we talk about temperature, low is a relative term. In this case, _____

_____.

These specifics can only be met in two types of places. One is _____

_____.

The type of diamonds that are formed in these impact craters, however, are usually quite

small and _____ microdiamonds. The other location is in the

earth's, um... lithospheric mantle. These regions are known as cratons, and they are found

in the thick, stable sections of continental plates, _____

_____.

Now, any diamond that is formed in a craton _____

_____... and there it will remain, perhaps for

billions of years, until something brings it up to the surface. So how does this happen? Well,

_____

that can take place deep inside of the earth. The magma involved in these eruptions is the,

um... is the melted form of a kind of rock called kimberlite. When these eruptions occur,

this molten kimberlite rushes to the earth's surface through tubular geological formations

known as volcanic pipes, _____

_____ and carrying them upward. These

diamonds are subsequently deposited in areas far closer to the surface of the earth.

iBT Practice 01

TOEFL Listening

VOLUME HELP OK NEXT

Note-Taking

1. Why does the student go to see the professor?
   - (A) To request feedback on her paper
   - (B) To drop her current classes
   - (C) To ask about her academic plan
   - (D) To get an explanation of a dual degree

2. Why do the student's parents prefer biology to literature?
   - (A) Because they are not interested in literature
   - (B) Because they believe literature class costs more money than biology class
   - (C) Because they think it would take less time to get a biology degree
   - (D) Because they feel students with a biology degree can earn a higher salary

3. Which of the following is true of a dual degree?
   - (A) Students do not have to do minors.
   - (B) It is required for going to grad school.
   - (C) It takes longer to complete than a regular degree.
   - (D) Students have to take more core classes.

4. What is the student likely to decide to do?
   - (A) Change her major to literature
   - (B) Study literature in graduate school
   - (C) Request a follow-up Shakespeare course
   - (D) Do a dual degree in biology and literature

Listen again to part of the conversation.
Then answer the question.

5. What does the professor mean when he says this: 🎧
   - (A) He thinks the student needs to take a summer class.
   - (B) He thinks the student is making a rash decision.
   - (C) He wants to make the student take his literature class.
   - (D) He wants the student to study biology rather than literature.

● iBT Practice 02

TOEFL Listening VOLUME HELP OK NEXT

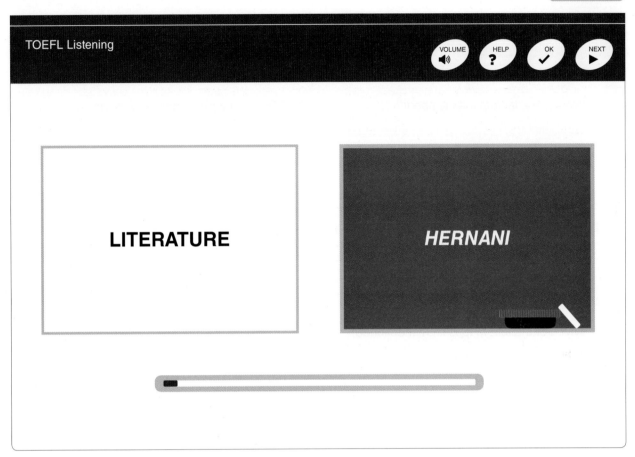

LITERATURE

HERNANI

Note-Taking

1. What is the lecture mainly about?
   (A) The creation of Classical standards in literature
   (B) Aristotle's influence on European literature
   (C) Why Victor Hugo's plays were unsuccessful
   (D) The advent of Romantic ideals in European literature

2. Which of the following is NOT mentioned about the three unities?
   (A) They were asserted by Aristotle in ancient Greek times.
   (B) They are the rules about time, place, and action in plays.
   (C) They emphasize multiple plots and passionate style in drama.
   (D) They had a great influence on European drama in the Classical period.

3. According to the professor, how did some English plays differ from other European drama before the nineteenth century?
   (A) They were not confined by Classicism.
   (B) They borrowed plots from Greek plays.
   (C) They were not well-received by the public.
   (D) They took place within a single place and time.

4. What established Victor Hugo as an important Romantic?
   (A) His leadership during "The Battle of Hernani"
   (B) The opening night of his play *Hernani*
   (C) His essay and play that rejected the three unities
   (D) A Classical drama he wrote in 1827

Listen again to part of the lecture.
Then answer the question.

5. What can be inferred about the student?
   (A) She has misunderstood the professor's question.
   (B) She believes there is more than one way to define the term.
   (C) She has taken a class about Romanticism before.
   (D) She thinks the professor's question is unrelated to literature.

Listen again to part of the lecture.
Then answer the question.

6. What does the professor mean when he says this:
   (A) He wants to emphasize the importance of the event.
   (B) He thinks the event he is describing is ridiculous.
   (C) He wants to hear the students' opinions about the fight.
   (D) He is worried the students are not paying attention.

iBT Practice 03

TOEFL Listening

VOLUME | HELP | OK | NEXT

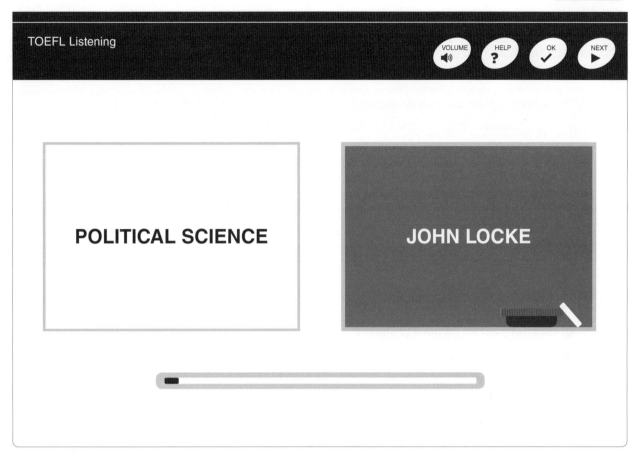

POLITICAL SCIENCE

JOHN LOCKE

Note-Taking

1. What does the professor mainly discuss?
   - (A) A comparison of beliefs about labor
   - (B) The philosophy behind a thinker's theory
   - (C) A history of modern property laws
   - (D) Methods of tending farmland

2. Why does the professor mention the idea that God intended for humans to share the world's lands?
   - (A) To explain why the ownership of private property was once prohibited
   - (B) To begin a discussion of common beliefs in the time of John Locke
   - (C) To question the fact that people were allowed to own private property
   - (D) To introduce a philosophical problem John Locke decided to resolve

3. According to Locke, which of the following parcels of land would NOT qualify as private property?
   - (A) A fruit orchard run for profit
   - (B) A grove of trees in their natural state
   - (C) A field of corn that has been harvested
   - (D) A pond that provides a family with fish

4. What limitation does the professor say John Locke placed on private property?
   - (A) The ownership of so much land that resources went unused
   - (B) The exchange of one type of product for a less perishable one
   - (C) The use of private property to earn money
   - (D) The hoarding of resources for winter

Listen again to part of the lecture.
Then answer the question.

5. Why does the professor say this:
   - (A) To give an example of what she explained
   - (B) To make sure that the students are paying attention
   - (C) To introduce a point of contradiction
   - (D) To signal that she made a mistake

Listen again to part of the lecture.
Then answer the question.

6. What does the professor mean when she says this:
   - (A) She wants to emphasize the main idea of the lecture.
   - (B) She thinks Locke's theory of labor is too general.
   - (C) She wants the students to focus on a specific point.
   - (D) She thinks Locke neglected an issue.

Vocabulary Check

- [ ] courtship
- [ ] mating
- [ ] sequence
- [ ] territorial
- [ ] parakeet
- [ ] initiate
- [ ] puff up
- [ ] interval
- [ ] tap
- [ ] beak
- [ ] pupil
- [ ] wooing

- [ ] idealize
- [ ] meticulous
- [ ] steadfast
- [ ] devotion
- [ ] synthesize
- [ ] abstraction
- [ ] representation
- [ ] depict
- [ ] mundane
- [ ] detached

- [ ] phenomenon
- [ ] transparent
- [ ] transparency
- [ ] condensation
- [ ] dew
- [ ] layer
- [ ] to make matters worse
- [ ] overpass
- [ ] facilitate
- [ ] traction
- [ ] slam on the brakes

- [ ] reschedule

- [ ] subterranean
- [ ] termite
- [ ] colony
- [ ] number
- [ ] caste
- [ ] delicate
- [ ] thrive
- [ ] susceptible
- [ ] forage
- [ ] vulnerable
- [ ] hydrated
- [ ] prevalent
- [ ] saliva
- [ ] secretion
- [ ] ingenious
- [ ] debris

- [ ] room
- [ ] variation
- [ ] in the neighborhood of
- [ ] meteorite
- [ ] slam into
- [ ] impact crater
- [ ] lithospheric
- [ ] craton
- [ ] eruption
- [ ] kimberlite
- [ ] tubular
- [ ] snare
- [ ] embed

- [ ] intro
- [ ] let sb down
- [ ] swallow
- [ ] to begin with
- [ ] talk sb out of sth
- [ ] grad school

- [ ] dual
- [ ] Bachelor of Arts[Science]
- [ ] burn the bridges
- [ ] core
- [ ] minor

- [ ] Romantic
- [ ] rebel
- [ ] rebellion
- [ ] Classicism
- [ ] Classicist
- [ ] school of thought
- [ ] convention
- [ ] three unities
- [ ] hard-and-fast
- [ ] playwright
- [ ] deliberately
- [ ] embody
- [ ] stir
- [ ] disregard
- [ ] defining moment

- [ ] property
- [ ] exclusive
- [ ] embellish
- [ ] alter
- [ ] constitute
- [ ] acorn
- [ ] acknowledge
- [ ] plum
- [ ] surplus
- [ ] possession
- [ ] perish
- [ ] squander

Vocabulary Review

A **Choose the correct word for each definition.**

depict transparent squander persistent synthesize prevalent

1. allowing you to see through it: _____
2. to combine separate entities into one: _____
3. to represent or portray: _____
4. to spend wastefully: _____
5. common or widespread: _____

B **Choose the best word or phrase to explain the underlined word.**

1. If something is <u>subterranean</u>, it is _____.
   A below average   B below the equator   C underwater   D underground

2. If you want to keep <u>hydrated</u>, you should _____.
   A do exercise   B eat a light snack   C drink water   D take a nap

3. An <u>ingenious</u> idea or method is something that is _____.
   A overdue   B clever   C mundane   D simple

4. If you are <u>vulnerable</u>, you _____.
   A can't drive a car   B have many friends
   C like to go shopping   D can be easily hurt

C **Choose the best word to complete each sentence.**

1. When we heat the house in the winter, _____ forms on the windows.
   A condensation   B solid   C layer   D vapor

2. People living near the volcano were evacuated well before the _____ so no one was hurt.
   A abstraction   B safety   C erosion   D eruption

3. Teenagers tend to _____ against their parents' belief systems.
   A apply   B forage   C rebel   D trust

4. The tires were completely worn and lost _____ on the wet road.
   A variation   B space   C view   D traction

D Choose the correct word to complete each sentence.

1. Many passengers died when the plane slammed _____ the mountain. (on / into)
2. He makes somewhere in the _____ of a hundred thousand dollars a year. (park / neighborhood)
3. I'm sorry I let you _____. I'll make it up to you this weekend. (down / out)
4. I know you don't like your boss, but don't burn any _____. You'll need to use him as a reference. (matches / bridges)
5. The bird was puffing _____ its feathers to make itself look big. (up / on)

E Choose the word or phrase that is closest in meaning to the underlined word.

1. He initiated the event by introducing the special guest.
   Ⓐ pitched   Ⓑ interrupted   Ⓒ concluded   Ⓓ began

2. This suite is detached from the main house with its private entrance.
   Ⓐ separate   Ⓑ embedded   Ⓒ combined   Ⓓ residential

3. There are no hard-and-fast rules here.
   Ⓐ flexible   Ⓑ accepted   Ⓒ strict   Ⓓ unreasonable

4. We took possession of the house after all the papers were signed.
   Ⓐ insurance   Ⓑ ownership   Ⓒ interest   Ⓓ care

5. She acknowledges that she becomes bad-tempered when she gets stressed out.
   Ⓐ alters   Ⓑ idealizes   Ⓒ embellishes   Ⓓ admits

F Choose the word that is the opposite of the underlined word.

1. He is meticulous in his research.
   Ⓐ innovative   Ⓑ conventional   Ⓒ careless   Ⓓ professional

2. Higher interest rates could hinder economic growth.
   Ⓐ facilitate   Ⓑ discourage   Ⓒ cease   Ⓓ worsen

3. He is susceptible to the disease.
   Ⓐ obedient   Ⓑ resistant   Ⓒ exposed   Ⓓ allergic

Pragmatic Understanding Questions

Function

Introduction

- Function questions focus on the speaker's reason for talking about particular information.
- These questions are often presented in Replay format, along with a relevant excerpt from the passage.
- 1 to 2 questions are presented for each passage.

Question Types

- Why does the student say this: 🎧
- What does the professor mean when he/she says this: 🎧
- What does the professor imply when he/she says this: 🎧

Strategy

1. Figure out the intentions of the speaker in a given situation.

   Remember that one expression can have different meanings in different contexts. Therefore, don't simply interpret the speaker's statement; think about what the speaker means given the overall situation. For example, the statement "It sure is hot in here" might mean the speaker is simply hot, but if a guest says it while sweating, the speaker could be suggesting that he/she would like to have the air conditioner switched on.

2. For questions asking about the reason why the speaker has said something, answer choices have such phrases as: to suggest, to recommend, to advise, to complain, to apologize, to accept, to question, to give directions, etc.

Basic Drills

Listen again to part of the lecture. Then answer the question.

1   Why does the professor say this: 🎧

   (A) To cite more examples
   (B) To stress the topic of the lecture
   (C) To correct a misconception
   (D) To introduce an opposing idea

Listen again to part of the lecture. Then answer the question.

2   What does the professor mean when she says this: 🎧

   (A) She thinks the student did not concentrate on the lecture.
   (B) She thinks the student understands the term exactly.
   (C) She thinks the student should use a dictionary.
   (D) She thinks the student is confused with the two terms.

Listen again to part of the lecture. Then answer the question.

3   Why does the professor say this: 🎧

   (A) To explain why the name is given in French
   (B) To emphasize the positive aspect of the art movement
   (C) To show the connection between the name and its meaning
   (D) To offer the students opportunities to correct misunderstandings

Dictation

Listen and fill in the blanks.

1. A number of studies _____ how color influences our emotions and… _____ .

2. Meanwhile, _____ .

3. For this reason, weight loss plans _____ .

4. And the most romantic color, pink, is um… _____ . That's why this color is sometimes _____ .

5. Activated carbon, also called activated charcoal, _____ _____ between the carbon atoms and create an intensive surface area.

6. Surprisingly, _____ _____ a 150,000-square-foot field.

7. But, what I'm talking about is adsorption, which is, unlike absorption, the process of certain chemicals _____ .

8. And the bigger the activated carbon, _____ and the longer it keeps on working.

9. Now, according to Art Nouveau artists, an artist should work on everything from architecture to furniture design so that um… _____ _____ .

10. According to their credo, the beauty and harmony of everyday life is improved by the work of artists, _____ .

11. _____ the long-held, um… _____ between fine arts – painting and sculpture – and applied arts – ceramics, furniture, and other practical objects.

12. So, Art Nouveau _____ the essence and meaning of art… and to ensure that its obligation included, from that time on, any everyday object… _____ .

● Listening Practice 01

OFFICE HOURS

1 Why did the professor want to see the student?
- (A) To offer the student a job as a teaching assistant
- (B) To inform the student that she's been put forward for a scholarship
- (C) To discuss the first draft of the student's application for a scholarship
- (D) To encourage the student to apply to graduate school

2 Which of the following is NOT mentioned as a requirement for the scholarship?
- (A) A nomination
- (B) Good grades
- (C) Teaching experience
- (D) A statement of purpose

Listen again to part of the conversation. Then answer the question.

3 Why does the professor say this: 🎧
- (A) To give advice on the direction of the student's SOP
- (B) To describe the process of researching an SOP
- (C) To give a hint as to the correct answer
- (D) To encourage the student to reconsider the scholarship

Dictation 01

Listen and fill in the blanks.

Student: You wanted to see me?

Professor: Yes, come in. I have some good news. _____

_____.

S: Really? What kind of scholarship?

P: It's a full scholarship to do your Master's in business administration.

S: A full scholarship! That's fantastic! Then _____

at the restaurant.

P: That's right. _____ and you

will also be paid for your work as a teacher's assistant. You'll get practice teaching and

_____. What do you think of that?

S: Wow... I think it sounds fantastic. Thanks.

P: Now, don't start celebrating yet. At this point you've been nominated within the department,

_____. I will say,

though, that I think you have a pretty good chance.

S: What is it based on... like... _____?

P: Well, the first requirement, of course, is a nomination. That's taken care of... _____

_____. Second, you need

to have good grades. You've got those. You're not having trouble in any classes, are you?

S: No, not at all.

P: Good. The last thing is your SOP.

S: SOP?

P: Statement of Purpose. You need to write a letter _____

and what you plan to do after graduation. Basically, explain why you want to do graduate

studies and _____ in the future.

S: Hmm... it sounds like a tough job.

P: Well, think about the areas _____

_____. What you need to do is convince them

that it is in their interest to pay for your education. You do that by showing what you are going

to do for the field.

S: Okay, I'll get started right away. By the way, when is it due? _____

_____?

P: Sure, I'd be happy to help. The deadline is March 4th, so be sure to bring it by my office

_____.

S: Okay, I will. Thank you so much.

● Listening Practice 02

MEDICINE

---

1 What is the lecture mainly about?

(A) The link between globalization and the spread of the coronavirus

(B) The series of global events that led to the coronavirus pandemic

(C) The reasons people are choosing isolationism over globalization

(D) The ways in which the coronavirus differs from past pandemics

2 According to the professor, what are two likely consequences of ending globalization?

Click on 2 answers.

(A) A decrease in the number of future pandemics

(B) A setback in medical technology development

(C) A serious financial crisis on a worldwide scale

(D) An increase in unrestricted international travel

Listen again to part of the lecture. Then answer the question.

3 What does the professor mean when she says this: 🎧

(A) She agrees with what the student has just said.

(B) She appreciates the student's contribution.

(C) She wants the student to change the topic.

(D) She has read the same resources as the student.

Listen and fill in the blanks.

Professor: Let's talk about COVID-19, the, um, coronavirus. I think it's safe to say that the coronavirus pandemic has been _____ in the 21st century so far. While this crisis has brought people together in many positive ways, it has also led to a lot of finger-pointing. There have been _____ _____, one of which is globalization.

Student 1: Globalization? That doesn't make sense. How could globalization possibly cause an infectious virus?

Professor: Well, it's not _____. However, many people believe that globalization—or, more specifically, some of the things that globalization encourages, such as open borders, unrestricted international travel, and free trade—is _____ throughout the world so quickly.

Student 2: So what do these people want? Isolationism? That might sound good, but I don't think most countries _____.

Professor: I think it's safe to say that you and I are on the same page. Other people are taking a more measured approach. They're calling for _____ _____. Personally, I'm inclined to side with them. I simply don't see any evidence that globalization played a significant role in this situation. After all, _____, some far deadlier than this one. Way back in the 14th century, for example, the Black Death managed to spread from East Asia to Europe, killing nearly 200 million people along the way.

Student 2: Well, there certainly wasn't much globalization going on in the 14th century, was there?

Professor: Exactly. There was not. So it's not logical to suggest that putting an end to globalization will _____. And as for adopting a policy of isolationism, as you suggested, _____ _____. The end of globalization would likely mean the collapse of the global economy. Furthermore, it would make the, er, development and sharing of potentially important medical technology, such as new vaccines and innovative testing methods, harder to accomplish. Basically, _____ _____, the anti-globalists risk causing another.

● Listening Practice 03

ART

POP ART

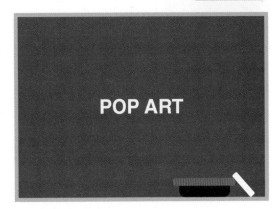

1 What does the professor mainly discuss?

Ⓐ The social background of Pop Art

Ⓑ The life and works of Andy Warhol

Ⓒ The differences between English and American Pop Art

Ⓓ The conception of the Pop Art movement

2 What does the professor say about Pop Art?

Ⓐ It was opposed to consumerism and mass culture.

Ⓑ It was based on the idea that everyone is an artist.

Ⓒ It tried to bring art into the boundaries of popular culture.

Ⓓ It revolutionized the way people appreciate art.

Listen again to part of the lecture. Then answer the question.

3 What does the professor mean when he says this: 🎧

Ⓐ He wants to encourage the students to participate in the lecture.

Ⓑ He thinks a contradiction in terms is apparent.

Ⓒ He wants the students to inquire about the contradictory statements.

Ⓓ He thinks the topic being discussed is controversial.

Listen and fill in the blanks.

Professor: Today we're going to talk about Pop Art. This was an art movement that began in the UK back in the late 50s... but... well... _____ in the US in the early 60s. But what is Pop Art exactly? We think of pop culture, also called popular culture, as kind of... kind of base... it's for the common people. But art... well, art is for the sophisticated... for the elite in society. _____, no? Well, this elitist nature is just _____. They were opposed to the serious and highly personal movement of Abstract Expressionism that was dominant at that time. And... Pop Art _____ _____.

So, how did Pop artists _____? Well, they did so by making art out of images taken from mass culture. Now, remember what was happening in the world at this time... this is post World War II, so _____ _____. The message everywhere is "spend spend spend." People had more leisure time as well, and TV was huge. _____ that Pop artists drew their materials. They _____ television, comic books, movies and all forms of advertising. Subjects such as soup cans, comic strips, product packaging, celebrities, hamburgers, and road signs were popular. At this point, I think I have to mention Andy Warhol. He is _____ _____. One of his paintings, named *100 Soup Cans*, is simply that... 100 Campbell's Soup Cans. Campbell's Soup, of course, is a major player in the soup industry and _____. The soup can is an everyday item found in our consumer-driven society. But... Warhol turned it into art. Warhol and his fellow Pop artists were _____ _____, particularly consumerism, by using popular images and icons and redefining them. By doing this, the movement made art closer to everyday, contemporary life. _____ between "high art" and "low art" and eliminated the distinction between the commercial arts and the fine arts.

iBT Practice 01

TOEFL Listening

VOLUME

HELP
?

OK
✓

NEXT
▶

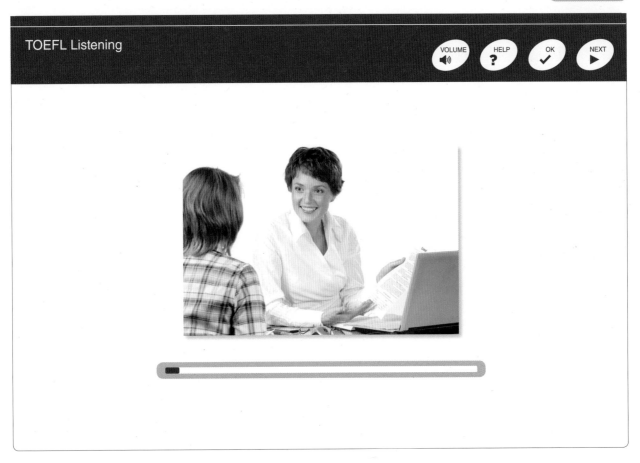

Note-Taking

1. Why does the student go to see the professor?

    A To discuss changing his major to archaeology
    B To pick up his essay on techniques in archaeology
    C To apply to volunteer in an excavation project
    D To ask whether he can receive extra credit

2. What is the professor's attitude toward giving extra credit to volunteers?

    A She thinks it is fair.
    B She resents having to do it.
    C She doubts if it will work.
    D She thinks it's an interesting idea.

3. What can be inferred about the student?

    A He will be too busy to take part in the project.
    B He will be chosen to take part in the project.
    C He will not have to take part in the training session.
    D He will convince his friends to volunteer.

4. What information has NOT been given to the student yet?

    A The location of the excavation site
    B The types of artifacts expected to be found
    C How many volunteers are required for the project
    D The volunteers' training schedule

Listen again to part of the conversation. Then answer the question.

5. Why does the student say this: 🎧

    A To imply that he assumes he will get the position
    B To insure that he does not appear over-confident
    C To request clarification regarding his status
    D To show his enthusiasm for the project

● iBT Practice 02

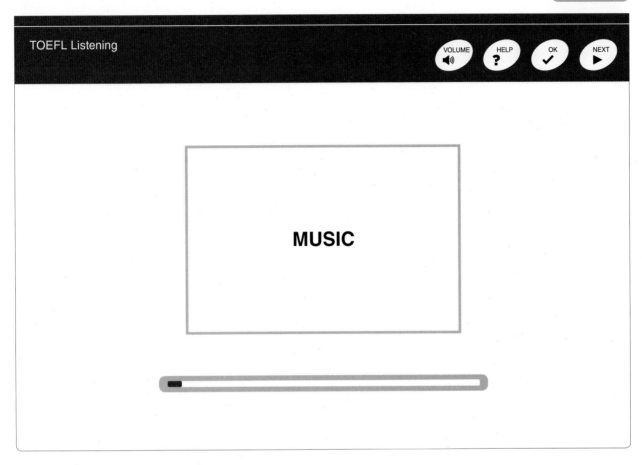

TOEFL Listening

VOLUME   HELP   OK   NEXT

MUSIC

Note-Taking

1. What does the professor mainly discuss?
   - (A) The mechanics and design of the piano
   - (B) The history of musical instruments
   - (C) The birth and significance of the piano
   - (D) The evolution of string instruments

2. How does the professor introduce the topic of the piano?
   - (A) By making a statement about its appearance
   - (B) By explaining why people love it
   - (C) By describing its sound mechanism
   - (D) By asking the students about their playing experiences

3. According to the professor, which characteristic was common to both the clavichord and the harpsichord?
   - (A) They had a wide dynamic range.
   - (B) They were unsuitable for being played in front of large audiences.
   - (C) They were the two most popular household instruments.
   - (D) They were the first instruments to feature keyboards.

4. What does the professor mention as the effects of the invention of the piano?
   Click on 2 answers.
   - (A) Making it easier to compose
   - (B) Contributing to the popularization of music
   - (C) Making it possible to express various emotions
   - (D) Holding a concert for ordinary people

5. What is the professor's attitude toward the piano?
   - (A) He feels it's easier to learn compared to the clavichord and harpsichord.
   - (B) He believes its status has been underrated since its invention.
   - (C) He thinks it enjoys too much popularity relative to its musical importance.
   - (D) He thinks it is one of the most remarkable instruments in music history.

Listen again to part of the lecture.
Then answer the question.
6. Why does the professor say this: 🎧
   - (A) To invite the students to give their opinion
   - (B) To reinforce the dual functionality of the piano
   - (C) To imply that the name is redundant
   - (D) To explain why the name was shortened to piano

iBT Practice 03

TOEFL Listening

VOLUME   HELP   OK   NEXT

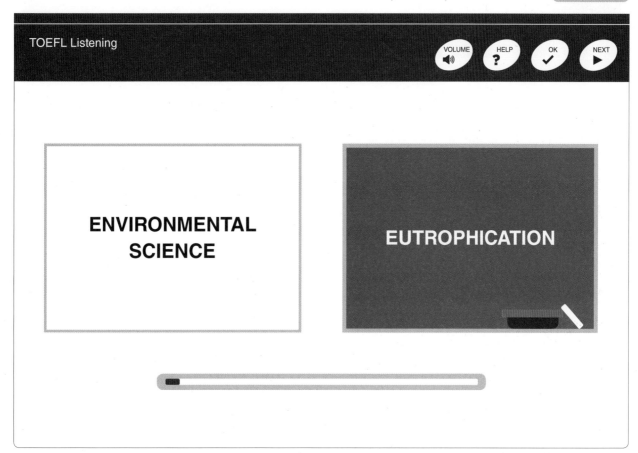

ENVIRONMENTAL
SCIENCE

EUTROPHICATION

Note-Taking

1. What is the lecture mainly about?
   - (A) The natural and artificial sources of chemical nutrients
   - (B) The process of removing nitrogen from water sources
   - (C) The economic effects of eutrophication
   - (D) The water pollution caused by excessive nutrients

2. What does the professor say about algal bloom?
   - (A) It replaces the native vegetation in water sources.
   - (B) It increases the amount of nutrients in water sources.
   - (C) It is a natural source of chemical nutrients.
   - (D) It deprives aquatic organisms of sunlight and oxygen.

3. According to the professor, what are the effects of eutrophication?
   Click on 2 answers.
   - (A) An increase in atmospheric nitrogen and acid rain
   - (B) The growth of some kinds of aquatic vegetation
   - (C) An improvement in agricultural productivity
   - (D) A change in biodiversity among aquatic species

4. What does the professor imply about farmers?
   - (A) They are the primary source of aquatic pollutants.
   - (B) They sometimes use more fertilizer than is necessary.
   - (C) They benefit from the eutrophication process.
   - (D) They are reluctant to use soil nitrogen testing.

5. What is the professor's opinion about eutrophication?
   - (A) Its effect is more serious than many realize.
   - (B) It should be reduced by completely eliminating algal blooms.
   - (C) It is a beneficial phenomenon when it results from natural sources.
   - (D) It should not be considered pollution.

Listen again to part of the lecture.
Then answer the question.

6. Why does the professor say this: 🎧
   - (A) To hint that eutrophication may have negative consequences
   - (B) To remind the students of something from an earlier lecture
   - (C) To make sure that the students understand the process of eutrophication
   - (D) To suggest that the effects of eutrophication are not fully known

Vocabulary Check

- [ ] evoke
- [ ] scheme
- [ ] stimulate
- [ ] suppress
- [ ] enhance
- [ ] temper
- [ ] tranquilize
- [ ] placate

- [ ] activated carbon[charcoal]
- [ ] pore
- [ ] atom
- [ ] equivalent
- [ ] innumerable
- [ ] adsorption
- [ ] adsorptive
- [ ] filtration
- [ ] fume

- [ ] evolve
- [ ] dismantle
- [ ] incorporate
- [ ] credo
- [ ] accessibility
- [ ] pottery
- [ ] customary
- [ ] obligation
- [ ] utilitarian

- [ ] nominate
- [ ] tuition
- [ ] requirement
- [ ] dean
- [ ] on behalf of
- [ ] submit
- [ ] impactful

- [ ] finger-pointing
- [ ] globalization
- [ ] infectious
- [ ] isolationism
- [ ] cut off from
- [ ] be on the same page
- [ ] collapse
- [ ] avert

- [ ] come into one's own
- [ ] contradiction
- [ ] elitist
- [ ] blur
- [ ] eliminate
- [ ] comic strip
- [ ] commentary
- [ ] contemporary
- [ ] consumerism

- [ ] excavation
- [ ] qualification
- [ ] introductory
- [ ] arch(a)eology
- [ ] fascinating
- [ ] artifact
- [ ] clay
- [ ] credit
- [ ] incentive
- [ ] delicate

- [ ] stringed instrument
- [ ] felt
- [ ] vibrate
- [ ] note
- [ ] wind instrument
- [ ] predecessor

- [ ] intricate
- [ ] mechanics
- [ ] dynamic range
- [ ] aptly
- [ ] alternate between
- [ ] interplay
- [ ] make a career
- [ ] virtuoso

- [ ] eutrophication
- [ ] phosphorus
- [ ] nitrogen
- [ ] to some extent
- [ ] drain
- [ ] fertilizer
- [ ] sewage
- [ ] choke up
- [ ] culprit
- [ ] alga
- [ ] algal
- [ ] discolor
- [ ] decompose
- [ ] deplete
- [ ] suffocate
- [ ] decay
- [ ] outcompete
- [ ] buffer
- [ ] interface

Vocabulary Review

A **Choose the correct word for each definition.**

| predecessor | stimulate | adsorption | credo | incorporate | vibrate |

1. to shake with repeated quick movements: _____
2. the beliefs of a particular person, group, or religion: _____
3. to include so as to make part of a whole: _____
4. somebody or something that comes before: _____
5. to excite or cause to act: _____

B **Choose the best word or phrase to explain the underlined word.**

1. If you have an obligation, you _____ do it.
   - (A) can't
   - (B) prefer to
   - (C) don't want to
   - (D) must

2. If you eliminate something, you _____ it.
   - (A) plan to use
   - (B) make use of
   - (C) get rid of
   - (D) can't stand

3. If you suffocate, you can't _____.
   - (A) eat
   - (B) breathe
   - (C) sleep
   - (D) see

4. If you tranquilize someone, they become _____.
   - (A) annoyed
   - (B) calm
   - (C) fearful
   - (D) thrilled

C **Choose the best word to complete each sentence.**

1. He shouldn't be around children because he tends to lose his _____.
   - (A) temper
   - (B) scheme
   - (C) commentary
   - (D) interplay

2. I have to take out a student loan to pay for my _____.
   - (A) scholarship
   - (B) excavation
   - (C) artifacts
   - (D) tuition

3. We must do something to _____ the existing barriers for disabled people.
   - (A) nominate
   - (B) submit
   - (C) dismantle
   - (D) outcompete

4. Talks will be held today in a final attempt to _____ strike action.
   - (A) restore
   - (B) avert
   - (C) blur
   - (D) notice

D Choose the correct word to complete each sentence.

1. I'd like to thank you _____ behalf of everyone here. (for / on)
2. We're going to alternate _____ the two. (between / from)
3. They felt cut off _____ the outside world. (from / with)
4. He was right to some _____, but his theory still had its problems. (matter / extent)
5. The new operating system never really came into its _____ and was eventually dropped. (hold / own)

E Choose the word or phrase that is closest in meaning to the underlined word.

1. Wearing kilts is <u>customary</u> in Scotland.
   (A) utilitarian   (B) mundane   (C) traditional   (D) cognitive

2. The game was <u>aptly</u> named.
   (A) appropriately   (B) ambiguously   (C) uniquely   (D) prematurely

3. Our graduates have <u>innumerable</u> opportunities for success.
   (A) perfect   (B) countless   (C) limited   (D) equal

4. Heavy drinkers are generally more susceptible to <u>infectious</u> diseases.
   (A) harmful   (B) restricted   (C) local   (D) contagious

5. The <u>culprit</u> got away with the money.
   (A) offender   (B) banker   (C) winner   (D) investor

F Choose the word that is the opposite of the underlined word.

1. The distinctions have been <u>blurred</u> in recent years.
   (A) faded   (B) ignored   (C) clarified   (D) denied

2. Fossil fuel sources are being <u>depleted</u>.
   (A) discovered   (B) decomposed   (C) circulated   (D) replenished

3. This movie brings together an <u>intricate</u> plot with well-developed characters.
   (A) modern   (B) fancy   (C) simple   (D) abstract

Pragmatic Understanding Questions

04 Attitude

Introduction

- Attitude questions focus on the speaker's feeling about or opinion of the content of the conversation or lecture, or about the speaker's level of certainty in connection with the information he/she is presenting.
- Sometimes, these questions are presented in Replay format, asking you to figure out the speaker's attitude based on an excerpt from the passage.
- 0 to 1 question is given for each passage.

Question Types

- What is the speaker's attitude toward X?
- What is the speaker's opinion of X?
- What can be inferred about the student?
- What does the professor mean when he/she says this: 🎧

Strategy

1. Use the speaker's tone of voice to recognize his/her attitude.

   A speaker's tone of voice gives important hints about his/her attitude. It may suggest emotion, preference, indifference, certainty, uncertainty, etc. Therefore, focus on how a speaker talks, not just what he/she says. Take care not to let important clues such as hesitation, emphasis, change in speaking speed, etc. slip by unnoticed.

2. Use the overall content of the passage to figure out the speaker's attitude.

   The overall content of the passage, not just one or two sentences, reveals a speaker's attitude. In order to successfully answer Attitude questions, understanding a passage's main idea and major points is vital. Pay attention to the flow of the conversation or lecture and put all of the clues together to make an inference about the speaker's attitude.

3. The following are commonly used expressions in Attitude questions.
   (1) Attitude/opinion: like, dislike, loathe, understand, be keen on, be offended, be interested, be surprised, be astonished, be amused, be hopeful, be impressed, be upset, be annoyed, be confused, be apologetic
   (2) Degree of certainty: sure, certain, uncertain, doubtful, confident, possible, impossible, probable, plausible, apparently, potentially, relatively

● Basic Drills

1 What is the professor's attitude toward smart grids?

    Ⓐ She thinks that they are too expensive.

    Ⓑ She doubts that they are actually smart.

    Ⓒ She believes they are a useful innovation.

    Ⓓ She hopes they are improved in the future.

2 What can be inferred about the professor?

    Ⓐ He thinks artificial reefs are essential for sport fishing.

    Ⓑ He questions the way artificial reefs have been researched.

    Ⓒ He is certain that artificial reefs help conserve marine ecosystems.

    Ⓓ He is not sure if artificial reefs are entirely beneficial.

3 What is the professor's opinion of green marketing?

    Ⓐ She thinks it has resulted in a decrease in product quality.

    Ⓑ She thinks it is proven to offer a wide variety of choice to general customers.

    Ⓒ She thinks it should focus on both environmental needs and customer satisfaction.

    Ⓓ She thinks it has contributed to raising environmental awareness among the public.

Listen and fill in the blanks.

1. It just refers to the network of powerlines that _____

   _____.

2. Smart grids _____ in homes and businesses.

3. Well, by anticipating peak usage hours, smart grids can _____

   _____ by minimizing waste.

4. Smart grids also _____

   _____, such as wind or water, into the main system.

5. An artificial reef is a man-made, underwater structure, _____

   _____.

6. Artificial reefs, um... in theory, have two potentials: enhancing sport fishing by aggregating

   fish and, simultaneously, _____

   _____.

7. Actually, artificial reefs _____

   because they attract fish, thus making them easier to catch.

8. But, despite all the studies carried out on reefs for the past four decades, _____

   _____ or...

   merely congregate fish.

9. Green marketing is when a company communicates to the customers _____

   _____.

10. As environmental issues become the _____, the

    trend is for more and more companies to _____.

11. Most, well uh... that is the vast majority of consumers are more likely to be _____

    _____ or improved

    product performance.

12. Therefore, overemphasizing improved environmental quality of the product at the uh...

    _____

    in green marketing.

13. Success in green marketing can be achieved _____

    _____ as well as their obligations to protect the environment.

● Listening Practice 01

OFFICE HOURS

1 Why does the student visit the professor?

Ⓐ To apply for a position for a new project

Ⓑ To request a letter of recommendation

Ⓒ To ask for advice about his career choice

Ⓓ To find out when Dr. Grey will return

2 What does the professor suggest the student should do?

Ⓐ Ask for a recommendation from Dr. Grey.

Ⓑ Send in the application as soon as possible.

Ⓒ Try to contact Dr. Grey by email.

Ⓓ Take part in her research project.

3 What does the professor imply when she says this:

Ⓐ She wants the student to be more confident.

Ⓑ She thinks the student has enough experience.

Ⓒ She is uncertain if the student will be hired.

Ⓓ She does not want the student to apply for the job.

Listen and fill in the blanks.

Student: Professor Starr? Um... _____.

Professor: Sure, Steven. What is it?

S: I'm applying for a job at Newton Laboratories. They're one of the biggest companies in the city and I'd really love to work for them. So, um... well, _____

_____ if you could write me a recommendation.

P: Of course I will. You've been an excellent student.

S: Thank you so much.

P: _____ at Newton Laboratories and they're all very happy working there. However, competition for open positions can be pretty intense. _____.

S: Yes, I've heard that. But _____. I've gained a lot of practical experience through working in the college lab, even though I have no working experience. _____, I think.

P: Well, good for you. But... well, I'm curious _____

rather than Dr. Grey. The two of you have collaborated on so many projects. I would think she'd have _____.

S: Right, but Dr. Grey is _____ in Paris. I heard that she won't be back until next week. And I have to submit my application by this Friday.

P: Well, as far as I know, she is coming back this week... umm... this Wednesday.

_____.

S: *[a bit embarrassed]* Really? _____. But...

P: Well, how about this? I'll write you a recommendation, Steven, but I strongly suggest you ask Dr. Grey for one as well. As I'm sure you know, _____

_____.

S: Oh, that's great. Thanks, Professor Starr.

Listening Practice 02

BOTANY

RAFFLESIA

1 What aspect of the rafflesia does the professor mainly discuss?

Ⓐ Characteristics and classification

Ⓑ The significance of the host

Ⓒ The process of pollination

Ⓓ Structure and distribution

2 According to the professor, what makes the classification of the rafflesia difficult?

Ⓐ The excessively rapid growth rate

Ⓑ The unpleasant smell and harmful chemicals

Ⓒ The comparatively short life span

Ⓓ The lack of typical plant features and DNA

Listen again to part of the lecture. Then answer the question.

3 What can be inferred about the student?

Ⓐ He thinks the professor made a mistake.

Ⓑ He feels the rafflesia has an unusual feature.

Ⓒ He is curious about the smell of the rafflesia.

Ⓓ He is suspicious of what the professor said.

Listen and fill in the blanks.

Professor: Take a look at this next photo. This is a rafflesia, the world's largest flower. It's a parasitic plant that's indigenous to Southeast Asian rain forests and _____ _____ as its, um... host. Instead of performing photosynthesis, the rafflesia _____ _____. The bizarre reddish flower of the rafflesia can grow to dimensions as large as a meter in diameter, _____ _____. But even more extraordinary than the flower's appearance is its odor, which is most commonly compared to putrefying flesh. Who can conjecture _____?

Student 1: Maybe it keeps plant-eating animals away...

P: That's a logical theory, but not the correct answer. Rather than attracting bees with the sweet smell of nectar, the rafflesia draws carrion flies with its stench and pollinates through them. _____ from flower to flower.

S1: How strange.

P: _____. In fact, scientists had to create a whole new family in order to classify the rafflesia, _____ _____ any pre-existing category.

Student 2: Why? Because of its extraordinary size?

P: No, not exactly, but rather because it doesn't have leaves, roots, or a stem, which are...

_____.

In addition, rafflesia lacks the genes most commonly used to trace plant ancestry, so _____. But... recent genetic analysis of the rafflesia's DNA determined that, um, it belongs to the same family as the rubber tree... despite the fact that all the other plants in this family have extremely small flowers.

S1: If so... how come only the rafflesia is so big?

P: Well, millions of years ago, the flowers of the rafflesia family were apparently only a couple of millimeters across... but _____ when attracting insects for pollination, allowing their odor to be more widely distributed and... making them easier to spot on the crowded floor of the rain forest. Consequently, they underwent rapid evolution... _____.

● Listening Practice 03

MUSIC

1 What is the lecture mainly about?

(A) The influence of classical violinists on modern musicians

(B) The importance of the Cannon in violin practice

(C) The musicians who switched from classical to jazz

(D) The first non-classical musician to play the Cannon

2 Which of the following is NOT mentioned about the Cannon?

(A) It was named after a specific piece of music.

(B) It was once owned by a famous baroque musician.

(C) It has been played by only a few musicians.

(D) It is proudly housed in Genoa.

Listen again to part of the lecture. Then answer the question.

3 What can be inferred about the professor?

(A) She doesn't think Carter was qualified to play the Cannon.

(B) She doubts Carter was the first black person who played the Cannon.

(C) She wants to emphasize Carter was both a jazz and classical musician.

(D) She thinks it was a great honor for Carter to play the Cannon.

PART B

UNIT 04 ATTITUDE

Listen and fill in the blanks.

Professor: Continuing our lessons on jazz and contemporary music, _____

_____ by the name of Regina Carter. And, I can... I can

_____ that you're familiar with her work. Regina

Carter is, of course, a modern jazz musician. A musical prodigy, she began playing the

violin at the age of 4 with the intent of becoming a classical violinist, _____

_____.

Now the reason I brought up Ms. Carter... is the, um, fact that due to her reputation as an

outstanding jazz violinist, _____

_____ – a chance to play the Cannon, the legendary hand-crafted

violin, made in Italy more than 260 years ago. Now, the Cannon _____

_____, and is not an instrument

for the faint-hearted. Way back in the 19th century it belonged to the great Paganini,

_____, and since then... the

uh... the proud citizens of Genoa, which is where the Cannon is kept, _____

_____. Okay, now getting back to Carter, um,

some people feared _____,

but the concert Carter played was a great success. In addition, she was given a chance to

record her album with the Cannon. Well, she was the first non-classical musician to play the

Cannon, as well as the first black person.

The reason it worked out so well, _____

_____, were the common traits shared by Regina

Carter and Paganini... that is, _____

_____ to play the violin. Classical baroque musicians such

as Paganini often used improvisation, which is also, as you all know, a main feature of

modern jazz musicians. _____,

although the music they play may sound different, jazz violinists and classical violinists

_____.

● iBT Practice 01

TOEFL Listening

VOLUME HELP OK NEXT

Note-Taking

1. Why does the student go to the snack bar?
    - (A) To make a group order
    - (B) To request time off during exams
    - (C) To complain about the quality of the food
    - (D) To suggest the extension of business hours

2. What does the manager mention as a possible problem for the student's proposal?
    - (A) Other campus snack bars will soon extend their hours.
    - (B) Students won't make purchases late at night.
    - (C) He can't ignore the policies laid out by head office.
    - (D) There won't be enough staff that are willing to work.

3. Why does the manager change his mind?
    - (A) Because the student has a very polite and favorable attitude
    - (B) Because the student's suggestion is likely to result in increased sales
    - (C) Because the student complains about the service of the snack bar
    - (D) Because the student is not willing to make compromises

4. At what time will the snack bar probably close during exam week?
    - (A) 9:00 PM
    - (B) 10:00 PM
    - (C) 12:00 AM
    - (D) 1:00 AM

5. Which of the following describes the change in the manager's attitude?
    - (A) skeptical → optimistic
    - (B) satisfied → doubtful
    - (C) concerned → relieved
    - (D) surprised → thankful

● iBT Practice 02

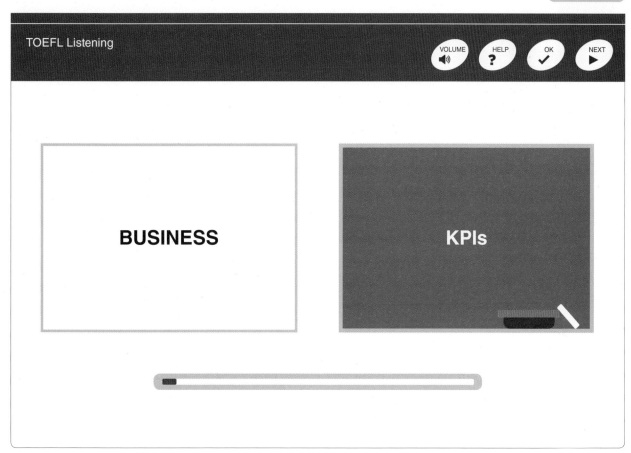

TOEFL Listening

VOLUME HELP OK NEXT

BUSINESS

KPIs

Note-Taking

1. What is the lecture mainly about?
   - Ⓐ Ways of measuring the health of a business
   - Ⓑ How companies share their data with each other
   - Ⓒ Two competing methods of analyzing businesses
   - Ⓓ Organizations that help improve other companies

2. How does the professor organize the information about metrics and KPIs?
   - Ⓐ By measuring each KPI against a different business metric
   - Ⓑ By explaining how they differ and how they are similar
   - Ⓒ By demonstrating how metrics evolve into KPIs over time
   - Ⓓ By presenting each KPI and the metrics used to calculate it

3. Which of the following is NOT mentioned as a type of KPI?
   - Ⓐ measuring the contentment of workers
   - Ⓑ analyzing the economic health of a business
   - Ⓒ charting the expansion of a company's market
   - Ⓓ considering the opinions and behavior of customers

4. What does the professor mention as a type of person who might use business metrics?
   - Ⓐ Someone who is seeking employment with a business
   - Ⓑ Someone who has been hired to provide outside guidance
   - Ⓒ Someone who is comparing the products of two companies
   - Ⓓ Someone who needs to find investors for a start-up company

5. What does the professor imply when he says this: 🎧
   - Ⓐ Metrics are rarely used by businesses.
   - Ⓑ Metrics are used by a narrow group of people.
   - Ⓒ Metrics aren't particularly valuable on their own.
   - Ⓓ Metrics could not be calculated without statistics.

Listen again to part of the lecture.
Then answer the question.

6. What can be inferred about the professor?
   - Ⓐ He is worried about potentially losing his own job to a robot.
   - Ⓑ He is an advocate of exploring the use of non-human workers.
   - Ⓒ He can't understand why people are unsatisfied with their jobs.
   - Ⓓ He doesn't expect a significant loss of jobs due to technology.

iBT Practice 03

TOEFL Listening

VOLUME HELP OK NEXT

ASTRONOMY

Note-Taking

1. What is the lecture mainly about?
   - (A) Theories about the origin of the Moon
   - (B) Prominent geological features of the Moon
   - (C) How asteroids affect the orbit of the Moon
   - (D) The formation of volcanoes on the Moon

2. What does the professor say about the Latin names for the dark and light zones on the Moon?
   - (A) They indicate Romans discovered the Moon.
   - (B) They suggest the surface of the Moon remains unchanged.
   - (C) They show a change of research methodology in astronomy.
   - (D) They reflect the misconception of ancient astronomers.

3. Indicate whether each of the following is related to the light zone, dark zone, or neither.

   Click in the correct box for each phrase.

	Light zone	Dark zone	Neither
(A) Was formed by volcanic eruptions			
(B) Is covered with many craters			
(C) Is a high altitude region			
(D) Is an ocean area			

4. According to the professor, what are the factors which cause the Moon to have many impact craters?

   Click on 2 answers.
   - (A) The lack of an atmosphere
   - (B) The absence of water
   - (C) Radical changes in temperature
   - (D) Very little erosion

   Listen again to part of the lecture.
   Then answer the question.

5. Why does the student say this: 🎧
   - (A) To explain the premise of the question
   - (B) To identify the professor's mistake
   - (C) To redirect the professor's question
   - (D) To query the professor's explanation

   Listen again to part of the lecture.
   Then answer the question.

6. What can be inferred about the student?
   - (A) He thinks the question has no answer.
   - (B) He is somewhat surprised by the question.
   - (C) He is unwilling to answer the question.
   - (D) He is sure of the purpose of the question.

Vocabulary Check

- [ ] apt
- [ ] meter
- [ ] minimize
- [ ] alternative
- [ ] crucial
- [ ] shift away from
- [ ] fossil fuels
- [ ] pollutant

- [ ] habitat
- [ ] aggregate
- [ ] simultaneously
- [ ] stock
- [ ] debatable
- [ ] congregate

- [ ] green
- [ ] jump on the bandwagon
- [ ] pitfall
- [ ] niche
- [ ] desirable
- [ ] overemphasize
- [ ] at the expense of

- [ ] recommendation
- [ ] acquaintance
- [ ] laboratory
- [ ] intense
- [ ] applicant
- [ ] shot
- [ ] collaborate

- [ ] parasitic
- [ ] indigenous
- [ ] grapevine
- [ ] host

- [ ] bizarre
- [ ] dimension
- [ ] putrefy
- [ ] conjecture
- [ ] carrion
- [ ] stench
- [ ] pollinate
- [ ] pollination
- [ ] lure
- [ ] unwittingly
- [ ] pollen
- [ ] trace
- [ ] ancestry
- [ ] undergo

- [ ] contemporary
- [ ] prodigy
- [ ] hand-crafted
- [ ] sonorous
- [ ] anecdote
- [ ] variation
- [ ] improvisation

- [ ] substantial
- [ ] arbitrarily
- [ ] feasible
- [ ] staff
- [ ] petition
- [ ] compromise

- [ ] metrics
- [ ] analyze
- [ ] statistics
- [ ] indicator
- [ ] get the ball rolling
- [ ] divulge

- [ ] retention
- [ ] internal
- [ ] utilization
- [ ] optimize

- [ ] discern
- [ ] mottled
- [ ] patch
- [ ] misnomer
- [ ] gaze
- [ ] erroneously
- [ ] riddled with
- [ ] crater
- [ ] comet
- [ ] asteroid
- [ ] velocity
- [ ] eon
- [ ] solidify
- [ ] destined
- [ ] friction
- [ ] erosion
- [ ] erode
- [ ] flux
- [ ] prominent

Vocabulary Review

A   **Choose the correct word for each definition.**

> simultaneously   putrefy   conjecture   preferably   optimize   analyze

1. to make something as good as possible: _____
2. to make a guess or theorize: _____
3. to study something in a systematic and careful way: _____
4. to rot or decay, creating an offensive odor: _____
5. at the same time: _____

B   **Choose the best word or phrase to explain the underlined word.**

1. If something is controversial, people _____ on it.
   - (A) work together
   - (B) avoid discussion
   - (C) disagree
   - (D) compromise

2. If you wear a bizarre costume, you wear something _____.
   - (A) contemporary
   - (B) beautiful
   - (C) weird
   - (D) national

3. If you choose something arbitrarily, you choose it _____.
   - (A) thoroughly
   - (B) randomly
   - (C) hurriedly
   - (D) habitually

4. When two people are collaborating, they are _____.
   - (A) entering a contract
   - (B) under threat
   - (C) in disagreement
   - (D) working together

C   **Choose the best word to complete each sentence.**

1. Environmentalists are concerned about CO_2 _____.
   - (A) dimensions
   - (B) biospheres
   - (C) emissions
   - (D) stocks

2. We should have advised him on the potential _____ of buying a used car.
   - (A) forums
   - (B) pitfalls
   - (C) improvisations
   - (D) prodigies

3. Spammers send thousands of emails to _____ people into buying their products.
   - (A) trace
   - (B) discern
   - (C) lure
   - (D) modify

4. I signed a _____ for building a new library for children.
   - (A) niche
   - (B) petition
   - (C) variation
   - (D) session

D **Choose the correct word to complete each sentence.**

1. They decided to increase profit at the _____ of the employees. (expense / charge)
2. More companies are jumping on the _____ and advertising organic products. (vehicle / bandwagon)
3. I can _____ my ancestry back to Eastern Europe. (trace / make)
4. The area was covered in _____ lava after the eruption. (destined / molten)

E **Choose the word or phrase that is closest in meaning to the underlined word.**

1. Your new plan seems feasible.
   - (A) ridiculous
   - (B) important
   - (C) debatable
   - (D) possible

2. He used an anecdote to demonstrate his point.
   - (A) evidence
   - (B) flowchart
   - (C) story
   - (D) journal article

3. The indigenous people of the land were displaced by the settlers.
   - (A) native
   - (B) foreign
   - (C) ordinary
   - (D) agricultural

4. He unwittingly let the cat out when he was taking boxes out to the car.
   - (A) lovingly
   - (B) foolishly
   - (C) deliberately
   - (D) unintentionally

5. There is intense competition among the insurance companies to woo customers.
   - (A) inherent
   - (B) fierce
   - (C) desirable
   - (D) sonorous

6. Price will be a crucial factor in the success of this new product.
   - (A) risky
   - (B) important
   - (C) trivial
   - (D) negotiable

F **Choose the word that is the opposite of the underlined word.**

1. The waiter erroneously told the chef the patron wanted his steak rare.
   - (A) correctly
   - (B) carelessly
   - (C) jokingly
   - (D) strongly

2. You mustn't pour grease down the drain because it will solidify and clog it.
   - (A) explode
   - (B) transform
   - (C) stick
   - (D) dissolve

3. We have some particularly apt students in the class this year.
   - (A) decent
   - (B) skilled
   - (C) incapable
   - (D) needy

PART

Connecting Information Questions

Organization

Introduction

- Organization questions inquire about the link between a particular piece of information and the organization of the lecture as a whole. Their purpose is to identify the way in which the main idea and its supporting explanation are organized and the reasons for the speaker choosing this method of organization.
- These questions require the passage to be thoroughly understood; partial understanding of the passage is not enough to answer Organization questions.
- 0 to 1 question is given for each passage – generally lectures, not conversations.

Question Types

1. Question forms that ask about the overall organization of the lecture:
   - How is the lecture organized?
   - In what order does the professor explain the topic?

2. Question forms that ask about the relationship between a specific piece of information and the lecture as a whole:
   - Why does the professor mention X?

Strategy

1. Identify the lecture's point and how the speaker supports the main idea. Take notes on the overall flow of the lecture while remembering to focus on the following signal words.
   (1) Compare/contrast: in contrast, on the other hand, however, similarly, likewise
   (2) Cause/effect: because of, X is caused by Y, Y results from X, consequently
   (3) Exemplification: for example, for instance, such as, to illustrate
   (4) Chronology: first, second, next, then, later, previously, finally

2. Think about the reasons for the speaker choosing to include particular pieces of information. When you understand the connection between a particular detail and the lecture as a whole, it is much simpler to identify the speaker's reasoning for including certain details. Possible reasons that regularly appear as answer choices are as follows: to emphasize, to introduce, to conclude, to describe, to suggest, to explain, to give an example.

● Basic Drills

1   Why does the professor mention the appointment at the museum?

    (A)   To emphasize the importance of close acquaintances

    (B)   To contrast the maxim of quality with other rules

    (C)   To show examples of violations of the rule

    (D)   To illustrate useful information for making inferences

2   How does the professor explain Newton's law?

    (A)   By emphasizing the fundamental problem with inertia

    (B)   By demonstrating how objects move without changing direction

    (C)   By asking the students the meaning of the relevant terms

    (D)   By comparing the principle to a previous misconception about motion

3   How does the professor explain incomplete metamorphosis?

    (A)   By comparing the different types of metamorphosis

    (B)   By providing details about the process of development

    (C)   By describing the factors which control its process

    (D)   By giving examples of animals which undergo metamorphosis

Listen and fill in the blanks.

1. _____, interlocutors have to _____
_____ besides uh... language
itself, like vocabulary or grammar.

2. This is about... it's about saying what's required, _____
_____.

3. So, more or less information than what is required in the conversation can uh... well it ____
_____,
and makes it impossible to have a truthful communication between participants.

4. According to Newton's first law of motion, inertia is the property of an object that _____
_____.

5. Actually, the... the dominant thought prior to Newton's day was that _____
_____.

6. He declared that an object wouldn't actually stop moving _____
_____.

7. But, _____ because this phenomenon
doesn't... just doesn't actually happen in the real world.

8. The book in motion eventually comes to a resting position because of... well as you said,
friction, and _____.

9. Now... _____, and we call
this developmental transition metamorphosis.

10. Next, _____.

11. Nymphs _____, but usually don't have wings.

12. As they grow, nymphs shed or molt their exoskeletons, you know, _____
_____ called chitin... and replace them with
larger ones.

13. _____, it will cease to molt and will
have grown wings.

● Listening Practice 01

> **EARTH SCIENCE**

1 What is the lecture mainly about?

Ⓐ The classification of rocks under the earth

Ⓑ A geological analysis of the earth's crust

Ⓒ A comparison between magma and lava

Ⓓ The formation of a common type of rock

2 Why does the professor mention cloud and fog?

Ⓐ To show how lava and magma undergo changes

Ⓑ To emphasize the importance of climate on rock formation

Ⓒ To exemplify the similar relationship between lava and magma

Ⓓ To illustrate the results of volcanic eruptions on climate change

3 In the lecture, the professor explains the two types of igneous rocks. Indicate whether each of the following applies to intrusive rocks or extrusive rocks.
Click in the correct box for each phrase.

	Intrusive rocks	Extrusive rocks
Ⓐ Are formed from lava		
Ⓑ Are fine-grained		
Ⓒ Crystallize slowly		

Listen and fill in the blanks.

Professor: Today, we need to briefly cover the topic of igneous rocks. These are rocks _____. Magma is subterranean molten rock, um... deep within the earth's mantle or crust. When this magma _____ _____, say through a volcanic eruption... we refer to it as lava. _____, but now that it exists under a different set of circumstances, we refer to it by a different name. It's sort of like when a cloud descends to the ground, _____ _____. It's now fog. Anyway... when this material cools down, it solidifies into igneous rock.

There are hundreds of kinds of igneous rocks, but _____ _____, based on the circumstance of their formation. Intrusive rocks, such as granite, are formed beneath the earth from cooling magma, while extrusive rocks – for example, basalt – are formed on the earth's surface from cooling lava. For this reason, extrusive rock _____.

And, among over 700 types of igneous rocks that have been described, most igneous rocks are intrusive rocks, formed beneath the surface of the earth's crust.

These rocks _____ by breaking them open and observing the quality of their, um, grain. Because intrusive rocks crystallize slowly in the heat of the earth's crust or mantle, sometimes _____ _____, the result is a coarse grain. Extrusive rocks, on the other hand, crystallize quickly – in a matter of days, in fact – as the lava is exposed to the earth's cool surface. Because of this, _____ _____.

Now, although they are not particularly evident on the earth's surface, _____ _____, you'd eventually see that igneous rocks are indeed quite common. In fact, they _____ of the upper layer of the earth's crust. And these igneous rocks serve a, um, useful purpose in that they can yield geologically valuable information on the make-up of the mantle and the conditions that existed there, _____.

● Listening Practice 02

BIOLOGY

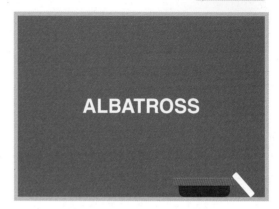

ALBATROSS

1 What is the lecture mainly about?

Ⓐ Surprising facts about the journeys of albatrosses

Ⓑ The impressive wingspan of albatrosses

Ⓒ Tracking the route of traveling albatrosses

Ⓓ The unique breeding habits of albatrosses

2 Why does the professor mention circumnavigation of the globe?

Ⓐ To contrast the migration habits between two types of birds

Ⓑ To disprove a popular theory about the flight of the albatross

Ⓒ To illustrate how the migratory paths change

Ⓓ To emphasize the long distance albatrosses travel

3 According to the professor, what is a disadvantage of dynamic soaring?

Ⓐ It burns up large amounts of stored energy.

Ⓑ It requires unusually large wing muscles.

Ⓒ It depends on the power of wind and waves.

Ⓓ It doesn't work during seasonal migrations.

Listen and fill in the blanks.

Professor: And then, of course, there is the albatross. The albatross is an extremely large seabird... in fact, one type of albatross, the great albatross, _____ in the world, with a wingspan of nearly 350 centimeters.

The albatross is renowned for its ability to, um... to travel great distances. _____ _____, however, the purpose of their journey is generally to seek out food. Albatrosses, you see, live on the open sea where food is plentiful, but when breeding season comes, they will _____, with each mating pair producing a single egg. When this egg hatches, the parents will take turns traveling for weeks _____, hunting for live fish and, um, other sea life, as well as scavenging for carrion. In fact, one individual albatross was tracked by researchers over a ninety-day period as it _____ _____. They found that it flew nearly 25,000 miles in that time span... an astounding distance, _____ _____.

Student: How can they fly so far? I mean, doesn't it _____ _____?

P: Well, first of all, albatrosses can store food in their digestive tracts, and they _____ _____ when they need it. This also allows chicks to survive for weeks without sustenance while their parents forage.

But more importantly, when they fly, albatrosses use an energy-saving technique called dynamic soaring. _____ and the ocean's waves to their advantage, which allows them to glide for long distances without flapping their wings. Because of this, the only time they really burn energy during these journeys is _____. However, reliance on this technique has left them physically unable to flap their wings for extended periods of time, _____. When confronted by calm seas and a lack of wind, a wandering albatross _____ _____.

Listening Practice 03

GEOLOGY

---

1 How is the lecture organized?

   (A) Seismic waves are compared to other types of waves.

   (B) General characteristics of waves are listed one by one.

   (C) Each type of wave produced by earthquakes is described.

   (D) Different types of earthquakes caused by waves are explained.

2 Why does the professor mention the speed of sound?

   (A) To emphasize the great speed of primary waves

   (B) To give students an example of a secondary wave

   (C) To explain why some waves are faster than others

   (D) To show how waves move through different materials

3 Indicate which type of seismic wave each characteristic belongs to.

Click in the correct box for each phrase.

	Primary	Secondary	Surface
(A) Faster than the other types of seismic waves			
(B) More damaging than the other types of seismic waves			
(C) Shake particles either horizontally or vertically			
(D) Move through liquids and gases, as well as solids			

Listen and fill in the blanks.

Professor: There are many things that move in waves, such as water, sound and light. But did you know that earthquakes move in waves, too? They do, and _____ _____seismic waves. Today we're going to talk about _____ seismic waves produced by earthquakes. Now... um, all of these, all of these waves, they move through the layers of the Earth, sometimes bending or reflecting _____ _____. The first type is known as primary waves. These are the fastest-moving of the three, so they are _____ when an earthquake occurs. _____ the Earth's crust, they move at speeds of about five kilometers per second, which is nearly _____ the speed of sound. They can pass through solids, liquids, and gases, and when they do, the particles of the material are slightly pushed together and pulled apart.

Secondary waves, as you might guess from their name, are the next waves you're _____ an earthquake. They're generated at the same time as primary waves but move _____. Unlike primary waves, they can't pass through gases and liquids—their movements _____ solid materials. And their effect on these materials is different as well. Rather than pushing and pulling particles, they shake them _____. Finally, we have surface waves, and again, their, um, their name gives you a clue _____. They move through the surfaces of the Earth, in contrast to the other two wave varieties, which _____. Surface waves are the slowest and most destructive seismic waves, _____ _____. Studying these different types of seismic waves has been very valuable to scientists. Along with _____ _____ the mechanics of earthquakes, they've also learned a lot about the characteristics of the Earth's interior.

iBT Practice 01

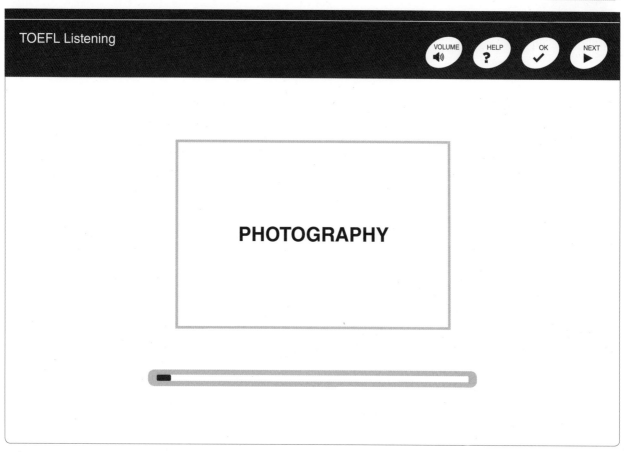

PHOTOGRAPHY

Note-Taking

1. What does the professor mainly discuss?
   A The basic elements of controlling exposure in photography
   B The advantage of manual cameras over digital cameras
   C The importance of being creative in photography
   D The correlation between shutter speed and aperture

2. How does the professor introduce the topic of a camera?
   A By showing its major functions
   B By explaining its basic mechanism
   C By contrasting it with similar equipment
   D By describing a commonly experienced problem with it

3. What can be controlled by changing shutter speed?
   Click on 2 answers.
   A The length of time the light rests on the photographic material
   B The sensitivity of the image sensor
   C The extent of the opening inside the lens
   D The expression of the subject's movement

4. What is the depth of field in photography?
   A The size of the aperture opening
   B The gap between the lens and the object
   C The amount of light that reaches the film or sensor
   D The range of distance that appears to be in focus

5. According to the professor, when is a large aperture useful?
   A When you want to photograph a landscape
   B When there is a large amount of light
   C When you want the background to be blurred
   D When the picture's subject is far away

Listen again to part of the lecture.
Then answer the question.

6. What does the professor mean when he says this: 🎧
   A He thinks manual cameras are superior to automatic cameras.
   B He thinks manual operation can add creativity to photos.
   C He thinks the students are unfamiliar with manual cameras.
   D He thinks the students should develop a personal style of photography.

iBT Practice 02

TOEFL Listening

VOLUME HELP OK NEXT

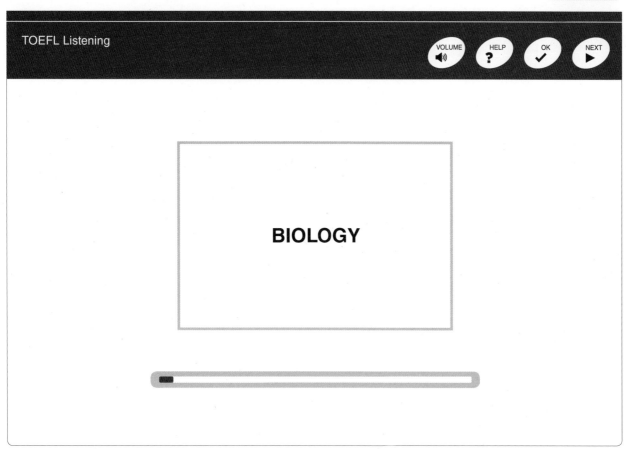

BIOLOGY

Note-Taking

1. What is the lecture mainly about?
   - (A) The effect of global warming on wildlife in the desert
   - (B) How desert animals and plants manage to survive
   - (C) The life span of animals and plants in the desert
   - (D) How desert animals and plants depend on each other

2. According to the professor, why do desert plants have such small leaves?
   - (A) To protect them from the hot sun
   - (B) To cut down on the loss of water
   - (C) To collect evaporated water
   - (D) To distribute nutrients quickly

3. Why does the professor mention kangaroo rats?
   - (A) To compare their metabolism to animals from cold climates
   - (B) To exemplify an animal that cannot survive in the desert
   - (C) To show a unique way of obtaining water in the desert
   - (D) To cite the results of a scientific study

4. According to the professor, how do desert animals protect themselves from heat?
   Click on 2 answers.
   - (A) By panting to lower body temperature
   - (B) By devoting more time to sleeping
   - (C) By covering their whole body in tiny hairs
   - (D) By sleeping during the day and being active at night

Listen again to part of the lecture.
Then answer the question.

5. What can be inferred about the professor?
   - (A) She wants the students to research the desert.
   - (B) She wonders if the desert is a worthwhile place to visit.
   - (C) She wants to talk about her experience in the desert.
   - (D) She thinks the desert is not a habitable place for people.

6. Why does the professor say this:
   - (A) To suggest what will be discussed in the lecture
   - (B) To encourage the students to participate
   - (C) To cast doubt on a common assumption
   - (D) To remind the students of the previous class

● iBT Practice 03

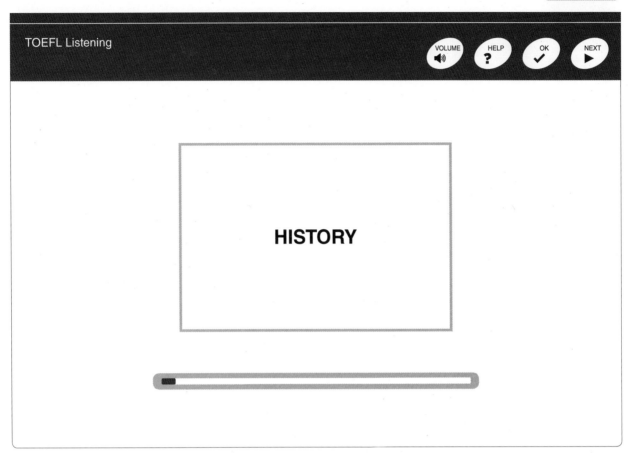

TOEFL Listening

VOLUME · HELP · OK · NEXT

HISTORY

Note-Taking

1. What is the lecture mainly about?
   - (A) The earliest calendar ever created
   - (B) How the Egyptians developed their calendars
   - (C) The importance of the Nile in ancient Egypt
   - (D) Why the lunar calendar was replaced

2. According to the professor, what marked the start of an Egyptian calendar year?
   - (A) The beginning of a lunar cycle
   - (B) The earliest sunrise
   - (C) The flooding of the Nile
   - (D) The sighting of a star

3. How does the professor introduce his description of the civil calendar?
   - (A) By talking about the structure of Egyptian government
   - (B) By calculating the number of months in a year
   - (C) By illustrating a drawback of the lunar calendar
   - (D) By discussing the extra period of five days

4. What does the professor say about the Egyptian's seasons?
   - (A) They determined the types of crops planted.
   - (B) They varied in number every year.
   - (C) They were used to schedule religious festivals.
   - (D) They matched the activity of the Nile.

Listen again to part of the lecture.
Then answer the question.

5. Why does the professor say this: 🎧
   - (A) To indicate that the student's answer is only partly right
   - (B) To explain that the origin of the calendar is unknown
   - (C) To shift the discussion to a different topic
   - (D) To praise the student for giving a correct response

Listen again to part of the lecture.
Then answer the question.

6. What can be inferred about the students?
   - (A) They have both misunderstood the professor's question.
   - (B) They have reached the same conclusion about the lunar calendar.
   - (C) The woman convinced the man to change his mind.
   - (D) The man is more informed about the issue than the woman is.

Vocabulary Check

- [ ] interlocutor
- [ ] maxim
- [ ] pillar
- [ ] hang out with
- [ ] hinder
- [ ] utterance

- [ ] inertia
- [ ] property
- [ ] dominant

- [ ] distinct
- [ ] transition
- [ ] metamorphosis
- [ ] nymph
- [ ] shed
- [ ] molt
- [ ] exoskeleton
- [ ] casing
- [ ] chitin
- [ ] maturity

- [ ] igneous
- [ ] lava
- [ ] subterranean
- [ ] molten
- [ ] spew forth
- [ ] now that
- [ ] intrusive
- [ ] granite
- [ ] extrusive
- [ ] basalt
- [ ] grain
- [ ] crystallize
- [ ] coarse
- [ ] fine

- [ ] account for
- [ ] yield

- [ ] wingspan
- [ ] renowned
- [ ] colony
- [ ] forage
- [ ] offspring
- [ ] scavenge
- [ ] carrion
- [ ] astounding

- [ ] circumnavigate
- [ ] digestive tract
- [ ] draw on
- [ ] reserve
- [ ] sustenance
- [ ] extended
- [ ] at the mercy of
- [ ] wandering
- [ ] wait out
- [ ] lull

- [ ] seismic waves
- [ ] crust
- [ ] particle
- [ ] liquid
- [ ] restrict
- [ ] interior
- [ ] destructive
- [ ] valuable
- [ ] mechanics
- [ ] characteristic

- [ ] magnify
- [ ] sequentially
- [ ] aperture

- [ ] expose
- [ ] exposure
- [ ] accomplished
- [ ] fraction
- [ ] blur
- [ ] frozen
- [ ] diameter
- [ ] depth of field

- [ ] harsh
- [ ] a myriad of
- [ ] inhospitable
- [ ] stride
- [ ] nourishment
- [ ] transpiration
- [ ] counter
- [ ] comparatively
- [ ] cuticle
- [ ] quench one's thirst
- [ ] succulent
- [ ] vegetation
- [ ] cactus
- [ ] flesh
- [ ] rodent
- [ ] subsist
- [ ] metabolic
- [ ] elevation
- [ ] dissipate
- [ ] pant
- [ ] nocturnal
- [ ] crepuscular
- [ ] dusk
- [ ] burrow

- [ ] calendar system
- [ ] address

- [ ] recede
- [ ] interval
- [ ] coincide
- [ ] employ
- [ ] formulate
- [ ] phase
- [ ] inundation
- [ ] overflow
- [ ] deficiency
- [ ] interlink

Vocabulary Review

A **Choose the correct word for each definition.**

| nocturnal | hinder | recede | formulate | undergo | inhospitable |

1. to move back or away: _____
2. unpleasant to live or stay in: _____
3. to be an obstacle to: _____
4. active mainly at night: _____
5. to develop a detailed plan: _____

B **Choose the best word or phrase to explain the underlined word.**

1. If you are an <u>interlocutor</u>, you are taking part in a _____.
   - (A) search
   - (B) conversation
   - (C) performance
   - (D) debate

2. If you go through a <u>transition</u>, you _____.
   - (A) change
   - (B) pant
   - (C) get sick
   - (D) become renowned

3. Your _____ are your <u>offspring</u>.
   - (A) parents
   - (B) siblings
   - (C) children
   - (D) employees

4. <u>Succulent</u> fruit and vegetables are _____.
   - (A) distinct
   - (B) nutritious
   - (C) sweet
   - (D) juicy

C **Choose the best word to complete each sentence.**

1. When you slam on the brakes, you continue moving forward because of _____.
   - (A) mechanics
   - (B) friction
   - (C) inertia
   - (D) metamorphosis

2. Ants live in _____ beneath the ground.
   - (A) colonies
   - (B) particles
   - (C) crusts
   - (D) interiors

3. I'm a vegetarian. I don't eat animal _____.
   - (A) pillars
   - (B) rodents
   - (C) vegetation
   - (D) flesh

4. The government has made great _____ in improving air quality in polluted urban areas.
   - (A) phases
   - (B) strides
   - (C) intervals
   - (D) elevation

D **Choose the correct word to complete each sentence.**

1. My mother said I can't hang _____ with my friends until I finish my homework. (up / out)
2. We can finally go to the restaurant now _____ the Smiths are here. (for / that)
3. After the boat's engine failed, they were at the _____ of the weather. (mercy / cause)
4. We can't go out now. We'll have to wait _____ the storm. (out / around)
5. I need something to quench my _____. (hair / thirst)

E **Choose the word or phrase that is closest in meaning to the underlined word.**

1. Members of our group follow a few basic maxims.
   - Ⓐ principles
   - Ⓑ leaders
   - Ⓒ properties
   - Ⓓ claims

2. This telescope magnifies images up to 20 times.
   - Ⓐ represents
   - Ⓑ dictates
   - Ⓒ enlarges
   - Ⓓ interlinks

3. She countered his argument with strong evidence.
   - Ⓐ supported
   - Ⓑ dismissed
   - Ⓒ discovered
   - Ⓓ opposed

4. He's an accomplished musician.
   - Ⓐ solo
   - Ⓑ retired
   - Ⓒ amateur
   - Ⓓ talented

5. It was a paradigm of the destructive side of human nature.
   - Ⓐ devastating
   - Ⓑ benign
   - Ⓒ favorable
   - Ⓓ skeptical

F **Choose the word that is the opposite of the underlined word.**

1. Canada has harsh winters.
   - Ⓐ dry
   - Ⓑ severe
   - Ⓒ short
   - Ⓓ mild

2. The wall is composed of relatively coarse sand grains.
   - Ⓐ heavy
   - Ⓑ bright
   - Ⓒ rough
   - Ⓓ fine

3. It didn't take long for the smoke to dissipate.
   - Ⓐ disappear
   - Ⓑ sink
   - Ⓒ gather
   - Ⓓ rise

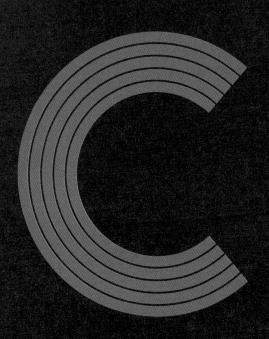

PART

Connecting Information Questions

Connecting Content

Introduction

- Connecting Content questions focus on the link between pieces of information in the passage.
- These questions require you to do one of the following three things:
  - Classify information
  - List information in order
  - Bring together information from different parts of the passage and draw a conclusion
- Tables and charts may be part of questions that require you to classify or list information.
- 0 to 1 question is given for each passage – generally lectures, not conversations.

Question Types

1. Question forms that require you to classify or list:
   - In the lecture, the professor describes X and Y. Put the following events in order. Drag each sentence to the space where it belongs.
   - Indicate whether each of the following is X or Y. Click in the correct box for each sentence.

2. Question forms that require you to synthesize information and draw a conclusion:
   - What is the likely outcome of doing procedure X before procedure Y?

Strategy

1. Briefly take note of the lecture's main idea and flow.
   (1) When the lecture is a compare-and-contrast description of more than two ideas, Connecting Content questions might ask you to classify ideas from the lecture. In this case, locate the criteria based on which you can categorize the given information and sort the content.
   (2) Connecting Content questions might ask you to order information when the passage is based on historical or chronological information. Focus on words that indicate time and sequence.

2. Similar to Organization questions, Connecting Content questions cannot be answered unless the lecture is thoroughly understood. Therefore, it is important to bring information together that is spread throughout the lecture and understand the overall flow.

Basic Drills

1   In the lecture, the professor describes how the Venus flytrap eats an insect. Put the following steps in order.

Drag each sentence to the space where it belongs.

   Ⓐ   The trap closes and remains tightly shut for a few days.

   Ⓑ   The insect touches trigger hairs.

   Ⓒ   The trap distinguishes between good and bad food.

   Ⓓ   The plant absorbs nutrients from its prey.

   Ⓔ   The trap attracts prey by secreting nectar.

1	
2	
3	
4	
5	

2   In the lecture, the professor contrasts the ideas of the Aesthetes with those of the Victorians. Indicate whether each of the following is a belief of the Aesthetes or the Victorians.

Click in the correct box for each sentence.

	Aesthetes	Victorians
Ⓐ Art should be appreciated simply for its beauty.		
Ⓑ Higher education is a goal we should all aim for.		
Ⓒ Art should make us better morally and intellectually.		
Ⓓ There is no purpose to art other than enjoyment.		

3   In the lecture, the professor describes how polar bears are perfectly adapted to survive in the Arctic. Indicate whether each of the following is a characteristic of polar bears.

Click in the correct box for each sentence.

	Yes	No
Ⓐ They have transparent fur for letting sunlight in.		
Ⓑ Thick layers of stored fat are used for energy.		
Ⓒ Short tail and ears don't radiate heat.		
Ⓓ They hibernate until spring.		

Listen and fill in the blanks.

1. First of all, with sweet nectar the plant _____.

2. _____, it is likely to touch one of six, short… and stiff hairs on the trap's surface.

3. If _____ enough to bend them, the leaves close down upon it _____.

4. But once the trap fully closes, _____.

5. _____, during which the insect is digested and nutrients are extracted.

6. For starters, you have to understand that Wilde was an Aesthete—that is to say, _____ _____.

7. The Aesthetes believed that _____ _____, an idea that was in stark contrast to the beliefs of the Victorians of that era.

8. They felt that we should all be constantly striving to, er… to improve ourselves, and that _____, teaching us moral and intellectual lessons.

9. Although they also valued art highly, they did so _____ _____.

10. _____ to keep warm is in their fur.

11. Actually, polar bears _____; they do not even show up _____.

12. Polar bears also have some special layers of fat, called "blubber," which help to protect, or rather uhm… _____.

13. Instead, they undergo a state termed "walking hibernation" _____ _____, in which their body functions slow down to reduce energy wastage.

Listening Practice 01

OFFICE HOURS

1   Why does the student approach his professor?

Ⓐ He needs the professor's permission to apply for a special program.

Ⓑ He wants to ask the professor to look over an application form.

Ⓒ He wants help in making plans for a study program.

Ⓓ He needs information for a project he is working on.

2   Indicate whether each of the following is what the student is going to do next.
Click in the correct box for each phrase.

	Yes	No
Ⓐ Complete a form		
Ⓑ Cancel a reservation		
Ⓒ Schedule a meeting		
Ⓓ Study for a test		

Listen again to part of the conversation. Then answer the question.

3   What does the professor imply when she says this: 🎧

Ⓐ The student's application form is late.

Ⓑ The student's hard work has paid off.

Ⓒ The student's grades aren't good enough.

Ⓓ The student's career goals are admirable.

Listen and fill in the blanks.

Student: Professor Walker? Can I ask you for some advice?

Professor: Of course, Darrel.

S: I plan on going overseas this summer as part of the college's study abroad program, _____. I'd like to go somewhere in Europe, but I'm not sure which country would be best.

P: I see. Well, _____ in Europe.

S: I've been considering France. I studied French in high school, and _____ _____.

P: Yes, Paris is wonderful. But it's the most popular destination for the program. There'll be a lot of competition, so the selection committee _____ _____. Perhaps if you had studied harder...

S: *[disappointed]* Oh, I didn't know that. *[brightening]* Well, what do you think about Scotland?

P: *[pause]* Scotland... hmm. _____ _____, but I have to say... it's one of the program's least popular choices. Most students want to learn a second language _____, and that's not possible in Scotland, as they mostly speak English. _____.

S: *[disappointed]* Yeah... Is there anywhere else in Europe where they speak French?

P: They speak German and French in Switzerland. _____ _____. And academically, the universities in Switzerland _____ in Europe. I've traveled there myself and really enjoyed my trip. I highly recommend it.

S: Wow, Switzerland... that's a good idea.

P: If you're interested, _____. Switzerland is not as popular as France, but _____ _____.

S: I'll head down to the Student Center after my next class and _____ _____.

P: Great. But don't forget, you also need to make an appointment to talk with a study abroad program coordinator. Until you do, _____ _____.

S: Wow, I almost forgot about that. Thanks, Professor Walker.

P: You're welcome, Darrel.

● Listening Practice 02

BIOACOUSTICS

1 What is the lecture mainly about?

 (A) The means by which a dolphin's brain processes echoes

 (B) The different forms of vocal communication among dolphins

 (C) The various reasons why dolphins are such social animals

 (D) The attempts by scientists to understand the language of dolphins

2 What does the professor say about the eyesight of dolphins?

 (A) Dolphins depend on it when hunting prey.

 (B) It becomes weaker as dolphins age.

 (C) Dolphins can see well but tend to rely on sounds.

 (D) Dolphins are blind and depend on echolocation to see.

3 Indicate whether each of the following functions belongs to whistles, clicks, or sound bursts.
Click in the correct box for each phrase.

 (A) To locate objects in the distance

 (B) To express emotions

 (C) To identify individuals

Whistles	Clicks	Sound bursts

Listen and fill in the blanks.

Professor: When we think of _____

_____, ocean-dwelling creatures might not

immediately come to mind. But dolphins... dolphins are extremely intelligent creatures that

use complex methods of vocal, um, interaction.

Now _____

in the wild, or perhaps at an aquarium, you know that they're constantly making some sort

of noise... and these noises, they all serve specific purposes. _____

_____, for example,

is one of their primary forms of communicating. Each dolphin has a, um, a unique whistle

which they develop at a young age. This is known as a signature whistle and it is used by

dolphins _____.

Then there are the clicking noises they make... short, sharp, _____

_____. In fact, dolphins have excellent eyesight,

but they rely heavily on the use of sounds because of the lack of visibility in their ocean

environment. The clicking sounds allow dolphins to "see" in this situation. Well, this happens

by... _____

_____, and the, ah, the time it takes for the echo to reach them, as well as

the volume at which it arrives, gives the dolphins valuable information about _____

_____. We call this echolocation, and it is especially

helpful when dolphins are hunting, _____

_____.

Dolphins also make what we call "bursts" of sounds. These various groans, barks and

other noises _____. A, um, playful dolphin

might squeak, while an aggressive dolphin _____

_____.

Well, this ability of dolphins to make vocal sounds provides us with fascinating research

subjects. One of them is about whether or not _____

dolphins use to communicate constitute a language. While there are those who believe

otherwise, _____, it would seem that the sounds

dolphins use aren't, um... well, they simply _____

_____.

● Listening Practice 03

METEOROLOGY

---

1   What is the lecture mainly about?

(A) Characteristics and types of tornadoes

(B) Predictions of tornado development

(C) Differences between supercells and tornadoes

(D) The origins and life cycle of a tornado

2   In the lecture, the professor describes the process of tornado formation. Put the following events in order.

Drag each sentence to the space where it belongs.

(A) The tornado absorbs warm, moist air and gets faster.

(B) The tornado is blown by surface winds and vanishes.

(C) A downdraft of cool air pulls the mesocyclone near the ground.

(D) A rope-like shape appears as the tornado meets cool, dry air.

1	
2	
3	
4	

3   What does the professor imply when she says this: 🎧

(A) Supercells reduce the potential for tornado development.

(B) Destructive tornadoes are associated with supercell storms.

(C) Most tornadoes are more powerful than supercell tornadoes.

(D) Supercell storms usually create landspouts or dust devils.

Listen and fill in the blanks.

Professor: Another type of atmospheric storm is the tornado. Tornadoes are columns of swirling winds that descend from storm clouds _____ _____. They are generally funnel-shaped, with an average size of about 150 meters across. Tornadoes themselves are actually invisible – they are, after all, just wind – but water droplets and accumulated debris caught up in their vortex give rise to, um... to _____ _____.

Okay, well... tornadoes _____ _____. First off, where do they develop? Well, tornadoes are spawned from supercell thunderstorms, which are storms that form from an updraft of warm, moist air _____. This rotation occurs due to encounters with wind moving in different directions at different altitudes. _____ _____ a mesocyclone.

Student: But Professor, isn't it true that not all tornadoes come from supercell storms... landspouts, for example, or dust devils.

P: _____. What I should have said is that most tornadoes are formed from supercells. There are exceptions, but they tend to be smaller, less destructive, and _____.
Now, where was I? Ah, _____
from a supercell storm, creating a, um, downdraft of cool air which pulls the mesocyclone closer to the ground. At this point, _____, elongating until it reaches the ground. Once fully formed, the tornado continues to grow by feeding off warm, moist air, _____.
This is the mature stage, _____ _____. But eventually, the warm moist air is replaced by cooler, drier air, and as the tornado loses its source of energy, _____ _____. It grows thinner, taking on a rope-like appearance, until it is blown away by surface winds and dissipates completely. At this point, _____ _____.

iBT Practice 01

TOEFL Listening

VOLUME   HELP   OK   NEXT

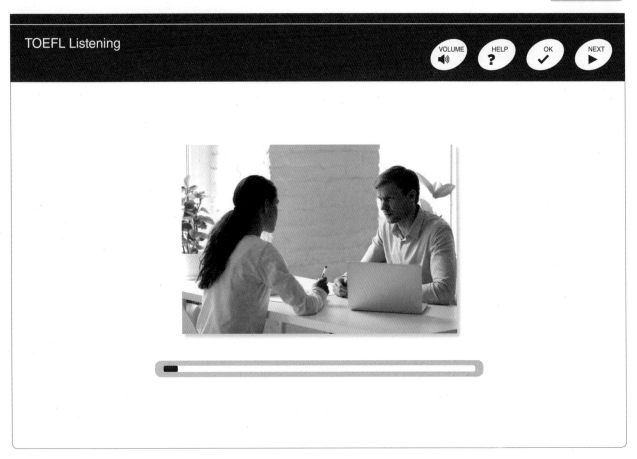

Note-Taking

1. Why does the student go to the student services center?
   - Ⓐ To complain about a problem with the plumbing
   - Ⓑ To reschedule her appointment to meet with the painters
   - Ⓒ To inquire about the cost of having her apartment painted
   - Ⓓ To check the status of a request she made previously

2. Indicate which problem is related to which form.

   Click in the correct box for each phrase.

	Green form	Blue form
Ⓐ A leaky faucet		
Ⓑ A broken heater		
Ⓒ Chipped paint		
Ⓓ Worn carpet		

3. Why haven't the painters painted the student's apartment yet?
   - Ⓐ Because she filled out the wrong form
   - Ⓑ Because she made a mistake on the form
   - Ⓒ Because she forgot to leave them a key
   - Ⓓ Because the form got lost

4. What will the student do next?
   - Ⓐ Take the painters to her apartment so they can begin immediately
   - Ⓑ Pick up her parents at the airport
   - Ⓒ Fill out a new form allowing the painters to enter her apartment
   - Ⓓ Schedule a specific time for painting

Listen again to part of the conversation. Then answer the question.

5. What does the student mean when she says this: 🎧
   - Ⓐ She wants the job done quickly.
   - Ⓑ She doesn't want strangers in her house.
   - Ⓒ She is frustrated with the long process.
   - Ⓓ She is excited at having her place painted.

Note-Taking

1. What is the lecture mainly about?
   - (A) How the English colonized North America
   - (B) The life of early American settlers
   - (C) The discovery of the remains of Popham
   - (D) Why the Popham Colony failed

2. How does the professor introduce the topic of Popham?
   - (A) By explaining why King James wanted to colonize the New World
   - (B) By asking the students to name early American settlements
   - (C) By contrasting its settlers with those that founded Jamestown
   - (D) By reminding the students of a popular story that involves it

3. According to the professor, who were the Popham colonizers?
   - (A) Pilgrims who founded Plymouth
   - (B) Spanish conquerors that were land holders
   - (C) Affluent Englishmen such as property owners
   - (D) Explorers who fought with the Natives

4. Indicate whether each of the following is mentioned as a problem of the Popham Colony.
   Click in the correct box for each phrase.

	Yes	No
(A) No medicine		
(B) No time to farm for food		
(C) Too cold a winter to endure		
(D) Warring Natives		
(E) Lack of a good leader		

   Listen again to part of the lecture.
   Then answer the question.

5. What does the professor imply when he says this: 🎧
   - (A) He feels it was an unfair act that England claimed land in the New World.
   - (B) He doubts King James allowed his subjects to move to another country.
   - (C) He is impressed by the passion of King James toward the New World.
   - (D) He thinks wealthy people played a minor role in English expansion.

   Listen again to part of the lecture.
   Then answer the question.

6. What can be inferred about the Natives?
   - (A) They had threatened Popham colonizers before.
   - (B) They broke off the contract with English colonizers.
   - (C) They had been mistreated by English colonizers.
   - (D) They were treated differently by English people than by Spanish people.

iBT Practice 03

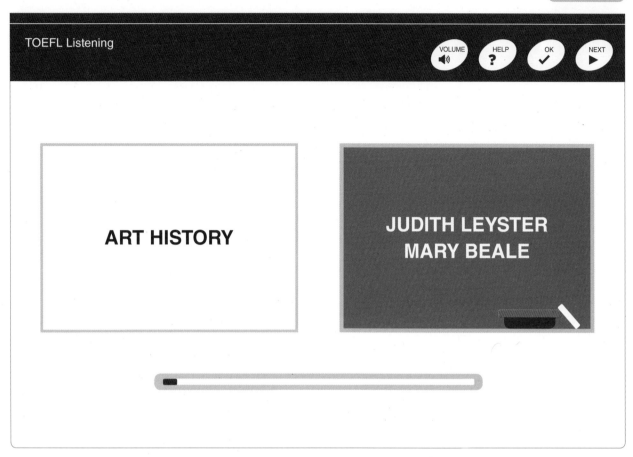

TOEFL Listening

VOLUME | HELP | OK | NEXT

ART HISTORY

JUDITH LEYSTER
MARY BEALE

Note-Taking

1. What is the lecture mainly about?
   (A) Difficulties overcome by the female artist Judith Leyster
   (B) The economic successes of women in 17th century Europe
   (C) Professional female artists of the Baroque era
   (D) Women's contributions to European art history

2. Why does the professor mention the Renaissance period?
   (A) To explain how the theme of painting changed after the Renaissance
   (B) To support the assertion that the status of women should be raised
   (C) To indicate that the change in women's position affected art style
   (D) To introduce the background of the emergence of female artists

3. Indicate whether each of the following belongs to Judith Leyster, Mary Beale, or both.
   Click in the correct box for each phrase.

	Judith Leyster	Mary Beale	Both
(A) Female artist in Baroque era			
(B) Came from a family of artists			
(C) Made a living by painting			
(D) A member of an artists' guild			

4. What can be inferred about Judith Leyster?
   (A) She was an apprentice to the female artist Mary Beale.
   (B) She was not well known among her contemporaries.
   (C) She pretty much stopped painting after her marriage.
   (D) She influenced her husband's career.

Listen again to part of the lecture.
Then answer the question.

5. What does the professor mean when she says this: 🎧
   (A) She thinks artistic movements that began in Rome typically affected artists working in other regions of Europe.
   (B) She doubts the Baroque era produced many works that had a long-lasting influence on the art world.
   (C) She thinks the students are already familiar with the Renaissance period and its impact on the Baroque era.
   (D) She believes the students now have the information they need about the Baroque era to understand the lecture.

Listen again to part of the lecture.
Then answer the question.

6. Why does the professor say this: 🎧
   (A) To express uncertainty and make a counter-argument
   (B) To support the student's idea and give a specific example
   (C) To change the subject and suggest new assumptions
   (D) To clarify the student's idea and introduce another opinion

Vocabulary Check

- [ ] Venus flytrap
- [ ] nectar
- [ ] seduce
- [ ] trigger
- [ ] primitive
- [ ] tripwire
- [ ] offending
- [ ] secrete
- [ ] acidic
- [ ] digestive
- [ ] extract

- [ ] aesthete
- [ ] aesthetic
- [ ] stark
- [ ] strive
- [ ] proclaim

- [ ] the Arctic
- [ ] transparent
- [ ] strategy
- [ ] detectable
- [ ] infrared
- [ ] blubber
- [ ] insulate
- [ ] hibernation
- [ ] scarce
- [ ] wastage

- [ ] grade point average
- [ ] coordinator

- [ ] sophisticated
- [ ] identify
- [ ] click
- [ ] high-frequency

- [ ] in succession
- [ ] visibility
- [ ] bounce
- [ ] echo
- [ ] echolocation
- [ ] school
- [ ] groan
- [ ] signify
- [ ] squeak
- [ ] be prone to-v
- [ ] constitute
- [ ] to date

- [ ] swirl
- [ ] funnel
- [ ] droplet
- [ ] debris
- [ ] vortex
- [ ] give rise to
- [ ] deadly
- [ ] spawn
- [ ] updraft
- [ ] tilt
- [ ] mesocyclone
- [ ] landspout
- [ ] dust devil
- [ ] stand corrected
- [ ] variety
- [ ] downdraft
- [ ] condensation
- [ ] elongate
- [ ] metaphor

- [ ] overly
- [ ] cosmetic
- [ ] plumbing

- [ ] skip over

- [ ] settlement
- [ ] presence
- [ ] aristocrat
- [ ] collectively
- [ ] presumably
- [ ] trooper
- [ ] successor
- [ ] inherit
- [ ] estate
- [ ] backer

- [ ] propagation
- [ ] suffice (it) to say (that)
- [ ] brewery
- [ ] guild
- [ ] apprentice
- [ ] esteem
- [ ] contemporary
- [ ] constrain
- [ ] breadwinner
- [ ] sitting

Vocabulary Review

A **Choose the correct word for each definition.**

> proclaim   extract   transparent   metaphor   esteem   acidic

1. to take out or remove: _____
2. clear or see-through: _____
3. to admire and respect: _____
4. an image used to symbolize something else: _____
5. to state something publicly: _____

B **Choose the best word or phrase to explain the underlined word.**

1. If something is <u>insulated</u>, it is kept _____.
   - (A) clean
   - (B) warm
   - (C) awake
   - (D) open

2. If something is <u>scarce</u>, it is _____.
   - (A) fascinating to study
   - (B) dangerous to use
   - (C) easy to figure out
   - (D) difficult to obtain

3. With better <u>visibility</u>, you are able to _____.
   - (A) eat more
   - (B) move freely
   - (C) see farther
   - (D) buy on credit

C **Choose the best word to complete each sentence.**

1. The person in charge of organizing an event is its _____.
   - (A) trooper
   - (B) backer
   - (C) coordinator
   - (D) adviser

2. These frogs _____ a poison from their back when they're attacked.
   - (A) secrete
   - (B) identify
   - (C) undergo
   - (D) inherit

3. I'm the _____ of my family, as I'm the only one who makes money.
   - (A) successor
   - (B) breadwinner
   - (C) contemporary
   - (D) founder

4. He devoted himself to the _____ of Christianity.
   - (A) wastage
   - (B) preface
   - (C) echolocation
   - (D) propagation

5. There's a problem with the _____. The toilet is backed up and the basement is flooded.
   - (A) downdraft
   - (B) nectar
   - (C) plumbing
   - (D) tripwire

D **Choose the correct word to complete each sentence.**

1. The animals escaped one by one in rapid _____. (presence / succession)
2. I am prone _____ get hay fever in the spring. (to / with)
3. I thought that was the case but I _____ corrected. (stand / stay)
4. His latest film is his best work to _____. (far / date)
5. Suffice it to _____, we won't return to this hotel again after receiving such terrible service. (say / know)

E **Choose the word or phrase that is closest in meaning to the underlined word.**

1. He was seduced into a life of crime by the desire to be rich.
   Ⓐ tempted   Ⓑ praised   Ⓒ lost   Ⓓ bothered

2. They are using sophisticated technology.
   Ⓐ outdated   Ⓑ useful   Ⓒ advanced   Ⓓ inferior

3. Her actions signify that she plans on making big changes.
   Ⓐ deny   Ⓑ indicate   Ⓒ recognize   Ⓓ ensure

4. He started off as an apprentice at the hairdresser's.
   Ⓐ expert   Ⓑ client   Ⓒ employer   Ⓓ trainee

5. Social divisions in the city are stark.
   Ⓐ meek   Ⓑ agreeable   Ⓒ obvious   Ⓓ uncertain

F **Choose the word that is the opposite of the underlined word.**

1. I can't elongate the telescope. It's jammed.
   Ⓐ modify   Ⓑ expand   Ⓒ contract   Ⓓ retain

2. The consequences of this oversight could be deadly.
   Ⓐ harmless   Ⓑ fatal   Ⓒ infrared   Ⓓ harsh

3. The police used handcuffs to constrain the suspect.
   Ⓐ interrogate   Ⓑ pursue   Ⓒ spawn   Ⓓ liberate

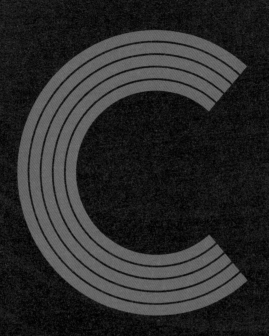

Connecting Information Questions

Inference

Introduction

- Inference questions ask you either to make inferences or draw conclusions based on information in the passage.
- Occasionally, the given question will appear in Replay format, meaning that a certain section of the passage needs to be listened to again.
- 0 to 1 question is given for each passage.

Question Types

- What will the student probably do next?
- What does the professor imply about X?
- What can be inferred about X?
- What does the professor imply when he/she says this: 🎧

Strategy

1. Make logical inferences based on the overall context.

   This form of question usually asks about suggestions or implications connected to the main idea or theme of the conversation or lecture. Therefore, you need to think about what might be logically inferred based on the passage's main concept.

2. Form conclusions based on information presented in the conversation or lecture.

   These conclusions must be logical and based only on the information in the passage, not on external information.

3. In many instances, wrong answer choices include words and phrases presented in the conversation or lecture. Select the correct answer choice that includes information indirectly stated in the passage.

● Basic Drills

1 What can be inferred about the color of the Golden Gate Bridge?

Ⓐ It was blended with many other colors.

Ⓑ It suits the name of the bridge.

Ⓒ It was chosen by unanimous decision.

Ⓓ It meets both aesthetic and practical needs.

2 What does the professor imply about meerkats?

Ⓐ They live only in groups to protect each other.

Ⓑ They are intelligent enough to give warnings of danger.

Ⓒ They attack others when they carry out guard duty.

Ⓓ They do not stifle their instinct for survival.

3 What can be inferred about beekeepers?

Ⓐ They have been inadvertently contributing to climate change.

Ⓑ Their warnings about a loss of bees were not taken seriously.

Ⓒ They are trying to control which flower species their bees visit.

Ⓓ Their bees are more affected by hot weather than wild bees.

Dictation

Listen and fill in the blanks.

1. Contrary to popular belief, the Golden Gate Bridge over San Francisco Bay _____
   _____ .

2. The name is in fact a _____
   San Francisco Bay.

3. Well, because the bridge's paint _____ ,
   the engineers and architects tested various paints.

4. It's also easy to notice for ships in the region _____
   _____ .

5. But this kind of behavior has been questioned by many scientists because _____
   _____ .

6. Now, if the meerkats' behavior was truly altruistic, the scientists reasoned, and I happen to
   agree, _____ .

7. And also if meerkats guarded for others, _____
   _____ .

8. _____ that meerkats stand guard when they
   have already eaten and _____ .

9. Now, however, it has been established _____
   _____ .

10. Although _____ , climate
    change is clearly a factor.

11. This is _____ .

12. If they were to suddenly disappear, _____
    _____ , including certain fruits, nuts and vegetables.

13. The bottom line is that we need the bees, _____
    _____ .

● Listening Practice 01

**SERVICE
ENCOUNTER**

---

1 Why does the student visit the office?

Ⓐ To inquire about local tourist destinations

Ⓑ To book a concert ticket for his parents

Ⓒ To find out the bus schedule to Red River Falls

Ⓓ To arrange accommodation for his parents

2 Which of the following is NOT mentioned as things the student's parents will do during this weekend?

Ⓐ Attend a jazz concert

Ⓑ Stay at campus accommodation

Ⓒ Change their flight schedule

Ⓓ Visit some waterfalls

Listen again to part of the conversation. Then answer the question.

3 What does the student imply when he says this: 🎧

Ⓐ His parents have a rare opportunity to swim.

Ⓑ He will visit Sunset Falls as well.

Ⓒ He will take his parents to the beach instead.

Ⓓ He is sure it will be warm enough to swim.

Listen and fill in the blanks.

Student: Excuse me, I want to get some _____ _____ for my parents. Is it true that students can arrange for family members to stay on campus when they visit?

Employee: It sure is. You just have to present your student ID.

S: Okay, here it is. And... _____?

E: That depends. If there's a conference or a workshop being held, _____ _____.

S: Is there anything planned for this weekend?

E: Unfortunately, there is. There's an environment conference going on on Friday, _____ _____. But Saturday won't be a problem.

S: Perfect! _____ on Saturday night and my parents are coming in from Scottsdale to attend.

E: Oh, _____! So, I'll book a room for Saturday night. Is that correct?

S: Yes. So, what time can they check in exactly?

E: Anytime after eleven a.m.

S: Okay, thank you. Uh... well... *[hesitating]* I was thinking about taking them to Red River Falls. I don't have a car, though, and _____. So, do you know of any other ways to get there? I'm sorry, I know you're not a travel agent and it's not your job to...

E: *[interrupting]* Oh, don't worry, we do this all the time. Red River Falls is a popular tourist destination so _____. I can write down the number for you. *[pause while she writes it down]* Here, you can call this number to find out the schedule.

S: Thanks. I appreciate it.

E: Oh, and by the way, Red River Falls can get pretty crowded. There's another waterfall nearby called Sunset Falls. _____, but it's beautiful too. You can walk there from Red River Falls... _____ _____ and the trail is well laid out with signs, so you won't get lost. _____, and you can even go swimming.

S: That sounds great. I will make sure that my parents take their swimsuits. *[satisfied]* Thanks so much for all your help.

E: Anytime. Just _____.

● Listening Practice 02

ZOOLOGY

SNOWSHOE HARES

PART C

UNIT 07 INFERENCE

1 What aspect of snowshoe hares does the professor mainly discuss?

Ⓐ Types of camouflage they use

Ⓑ Why they are becoming an endangered species

Ⓒ How they adapt to harsh conditions

Ⓓ Their ability to survive among predators

2 Which of the following is NOT mentioned as a survival strategy of the snowshoe hare?

Ⓐ Fur color altering according to the season

Ⓑ Underground burrows to avoid predators

Ⓒ Quick and swift movement

Ⓓ Digestive system that maximizes nutrition

Listen again to part of the lecture. Then answer the question.

3 What can be inferred about snowshoe hares?

Ⓐ They reduce energy wastage by hibernating.

Ⓑ They can recycle plant stems and tree bark to build their burrows.

Ⓒ They can live without any food during the winter.

Ⓓ They absorb necessary nutrients more efficiently than other animals.

Listen and fill in the blanks.

Professor: So, as we continue to discuss the various types of wildlife that inhabit the Rocky Mountain region of North America, I'd like to take a moment to talk about snowshoe hares. Well, _____, so they employ various strategies to survive such harsh conditions.

Firstly, their name is... as you probably know, _____ _____, which work much like a pair of snowshoes you or I might wear. They, um... they help the hares avoid their many predators _____ _____ without sinking beneath the surface. Besides, adult snowshoe hares can run at speeds of more than 25 miles per hour, _____ and high leaps into the air in order to avoid pursuing predators, _____ _____, if necessary.

Young snowshoe hares, however, are not as fast. When approached by a predator, instead of fleeing, _____ _____... because their fur, you see, is another important characteristic that aids their survival in winter. Twice a year, a snowshoe hare _____ _____. In the, um... in the summer, it's a brown color, but when the cold weather comes, long white hairs begin to grow, eventually becoming a new coat of white fur _____ _____.

Another crucial issue during these long harsh winters is _____ _____. Most plants die in the winter, and those that survive are generally covered in snow. But snowshoe hares can survive on nutritionally poor diets _____ _____. Importantly, the gastrointestinal tract of snowshoe hares can handle all sorts of plant material, and they extract all of the available nutrients from their food by cycling it through their digestive system a second time. As a result, while other plant-eating animals _____ _____, snowshoe hares can subsist on plant stems, pine needles and tree bark.

● Listening Practice 03

ART HISTORY

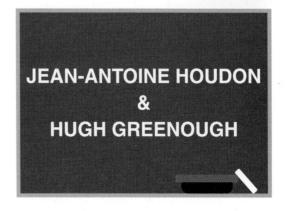

JEAN-ANTOINE HOUDON
&
HUGH GREENOUGH

1 What is the lecture mainly about?

Ⓐ Ways of appreciating modern statues

Ⓑ The public image of George Washington

Ⓒ The significance of Houdon's Washington

Ⓓ A comparison between two works of art

2 Which of the following is NOT mentioned about Houdon's statue?

Ⓐ It contains various symbolic messages.

Ⓑ It was extremely popular with the public.

Ⓒ It portrayed Washington as a Greek god.

Ⓓ It combined classical and contemporary styles.

3 What can be inferred from the public responses to the two statues?

Ⓐ The beauty of artwork is the most important factor in art appreciation.

Ⓑ Representing an idea that deeply connects with people is essential in art.

Ⓒ The location of a statue sometimes determines the popularity of it.

Ⓓ The appeal of a piece of art is often based on the reputation of the artist.

Listen and fill in the blanks.

Professor: When we think about George Washington, the first president of the United States, a strong image generally comes to mind. Now, if you'll turn to page 154 in your textbooks, you'll see _____ ... a photograph of a famous late 18th-century marble statue by the French sculptor Jean-Antoine Houdon. The subject, of course, is Mr. Washington.

This is a very popular statue, one that _____ _____. But if you look over at page 155, you'll see another statue of Mr. Washington, created by Hugh Greenough in the 1830s.

_____ Houdon's statue, to many Americans Greenough's statue doesn't seem like George Washington at all. So why does it _____?

Well, let's start with Houdon's statue. The style of the statue, along with the clothing Mr. Washington is wearing, _____. Mr. Washington is portrayed as a man, _____, with a plow in the background and a walking stick in one hand. His other hand... what can you see?

Student: There're 13 rods. I think they represent the 13 colonies.

P: Excellent. Actually, _____ _____. There are 13 of them to represent the original 13 colonies, and they are mixed with arrows, a symbol of the American frontier. In essence, Houdon _____, creating a style that Americans found appealing. Now let's move on to Greenough's statue. What is your opinion about it?

S: Umm... First, above all, _____. He's wearing an ancient costume.

P: Yes, Greenough portrayed his subject in the classical style. Mr. Washington appears as the Greek god Zeus, shirtless and wearing an ancient robe. He sits in an unnatural pose, with one hand held to the sky. _____ _____. This representation of Washington simply did not connect with most Americans, _____. Subsequently, it was moved several times, eventually ending up in a museum. Houdon's statue, however, _____ more than 200 years ago.

● iBT Practice 01

TOEFL Listening

VOLUME HELP OK NEXT

Note-Taking

1. Why does the student visit the office?
   - Ⓐ To apply for a position as a teaching assistant
   - Ⓑ To complain about a problem with the new computer system
   - Ⓒ To explain why she will be late paying her tuition
   - Ⓓ To report that she has not received her paycheck

2. Why does the student need her paycheck now?
   - Ⓐ Because she is moving
   - Ⓑ Because she owes a late fee
   - Ⓒ Because her tuition is due this week
   - Ⓓ Because her rent is overdue

3. Why couldn't the student get the paycheck on time?
   - Ⓐ Because she did not complete the job she was assigned to do
   - Ⓑ Because there was a computer error and her name was deleted
   - Ⓒ Because she did not fill out the proper forms
   - Ⓓ Because she did not hand in her forms on time

4. How does the student's attitude change?
   - Ⓐ Nervous → Overjoyed
   - Ⓑ Curious → Disappointed
   - Ⓒ Annoyed → Relieved
   - Ⓓ Grateful → Concerned

Listen again to part of the conversation. Then answer the question.

5. Why does the student say this: 🎧
   - Ⓐ To help the employee locate her in the database
   - Ⓑ To indicate that she is a current teaching assistant
   - Ⓒ To introduce herself to the employee
   - Ⓓ To try to rush the process along

iBT Practice 02

TOEFL Listening

VOLUME · HELP · OK · NEXT

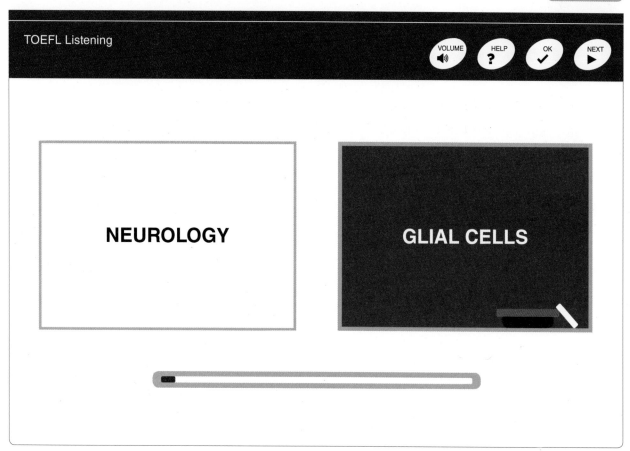

NEUROLOGY

GLIAL CELLS

Note-Taking

1. What is the lecture mainly about?
    - (A) How glial cells are formed in the brain
    - (B) The process of synaptic communication
    - (C) How neurons and glial cells are related
    - (D) The role of glial cells in brain function

2. According to the professor, what change has occurred in neurological understanding?
    - (A) It has been found that the composition of glial cells is unique.
    - (B) It has been discovered there is no correlation between neurons and intelligence.
    - (C) It has turned out that glial cells play many essential roles in brain function.
    - (D) The total number of neurons and glial cells has been revealed.

3. Which of the following is NOT mentioned as a function of glial cells?
    - (A) Physically supporting neural networks
    - (B) Sending signals across synapses
    - (C) Bringing nourishment to neurons
    - (D) Regulating the development of synapses

4. Why does the professor mention Einstein?
    - (A) To introduce an assumption about the relationship between glia and intelligence
    - (B) To contrast how glial cells and synapses are involved in neurology
    - (C) To emphasize the role of neurons in synaptic communication
    - (D) To illustrate the effect of medical examination on the number of glial cells

Listen again to part of the lecture.
Then answer the question.

5. What does the professor imply when she says this: 🎧
    - (A) It was believed there was no difference in size of brain.
    - (B) It wasn't expected that Einstein's brain would be removed.
    - (C) People believed smart people have a bigger brain.
    - (D) The brain of Einstein was no smaller than that of a normal person.

Listen again to part of the lecture.
Then answer the question.

6. What can be inferred about the professor?
    - (A) She agrees with the idea that the ratio of glia to neurons is fixed.
    - (B) She doubts the results of the experiments about glial cells.
    - (C) She thinks the contribution of glia to intelligence is still hypothetical.
    - (D) She believes high intelligence increases the number of glial cells.

iBT Practice 03

VOLUME HELP OK NEXT

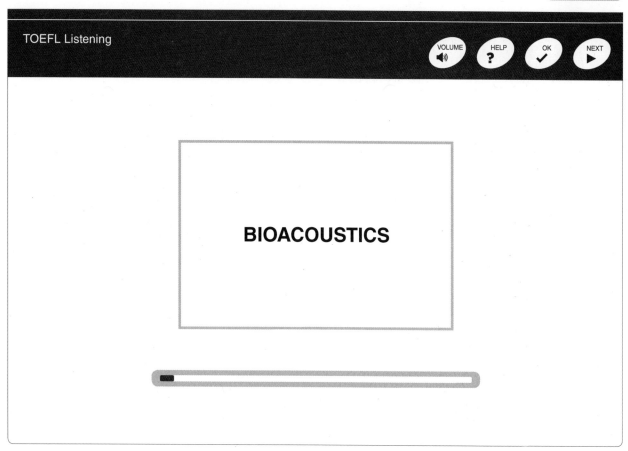

BIOACOUSTICS

Note-Taking

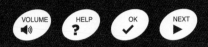

1. What is the lecture mainly about?
   A How elephants protect themselves
   B Different wavelengths of sound
   C How elephants make sound
   D The unique sound of elephants

2. Why does the professor mention cellos and violins?
   A To describe the sound produced by elephants
   B To explain the relationship between body size and sound pitch
   C To demonstrate under what conditions elephants make sound
   D To show how elephants react to musical instruments

3. Which of the following is NOT mentioned as a characteristic of infrasound?
   A It can be carried over large distances.
   B It is not easily absorbed by its surroundings.
   C It needs special equipment to be made.
   D It can be felt by humans through vibrations.

4. Indicate whether each of the following is related to low-pitch or high-pitch elephant calls.
   Click in the correct box for each phrase.

	Low-pitch	High-pitch
A Finding food		
B Facing a threat		
C Sheltering their babies		
D Looking for partners		

5. What can be inferred about elephants?
   A They can hear only low-frequency calls that the human ear can't detect.
   B They can make sound that overlaps with the range of human hearing.
   C They communicate with each other by using their huge bodies.
   D They produce infrasound and vibrations that other animals can't produce.

Listen again to part of the lecture.
Then answer the question

6. What does the professor mean when he says this:
   A He wants the students to review the lecture.
   B He wants to introduce a new topic for the lecture.
   C He wants to return to the main topic.
   D He wants the students to pay attention to him.

Vocabulary Check

- distinctive
- prospector
- via
- synonymous
- quest
- astonishing
- withstand
- azure
- suspend
- driving
- ultimately
- fabulous

- furry
- critter
- altruistic
- contradict
- inspection
- impending
- shrill
- retreat

- beekeeper
- die off
- adaptable
- species
- migrate
- pollinator
- ecosystem
- staple
- bottom line

- accommodation
- in advance
- trail

- inhabit
- snowshoe hare
- brutal
- be derived from
- freeze
- camouflage
- in one's place
- nutritionally
- digestive
- gastrointestinal
- tract
- starvation

- embodiment
- patriotism
- portrayal
- mythical
- plow
- rod
- awkward
- robe
- relevance
- subsequently
- erect

- paycheck
- tuition
- notify
- make out
- dispose of
- accounting

- analogy
- equate
- neurology
- neural

- transmit
- transmission
- synapse
- unfathomable
- scrutiny
- glial
- glia
- mind-boggling
- stability
- neurotransmitter
- filament
- misconstrue
- catalyst
- take on a role
- illuminating
- ratio
- indisputably

- infrasound
- infrasonic
- frequency
- audiospectrograph
- digress
- pitch
- wavelength
- calf
- scatter
- mighty

Vocabulary Review

A **Choose the correct word for each definition.**

> analogy   patriotism   synonymous   scrutiny   awkward   neural

1. very careful examination or study: _____
2. having the same meaning: _____
3. having to do with the nervous system: _____
4. love of one's country: _____
5. a comparison between two things that have similar features: _____

B **Choose the best word or phrase to explain the underlined word.**

1. If you <u>inhabit</u> an area, you _____.
    - Ⓐ conquer it
    - Ⓑ farm it
    - Ⓒ live there
    - Ⓓ vacation

2. If you are on a <u>quest</u>, you are _____.
    - Ⓐ staying up all night
    - Ⓑ looking for something
    - Ⓒ trying to lose weight
    - Ⓓ running in a race

3. If you <u>digress</u>, you _____.
    - Ⓐ give an example
    - Ⓑ slow down
    - Ⓒ get left behind
    - Ⓓ get off topic

C **Choose the best word to complete each sentence.**

1. This is my treat. I got my _____ today.
    - Ⓐ expenses
    - Ⓑ accommodation
    - Ⓒ paycheck
    - Ⓓ accounting

2. A monument will be _____ where the massacre took place.
    - Ⓐ withstood
    - Ⓑ erected
    - Ⓒ misconstrued
    - Ⓓ excreted

3. They were forced to _____ from rural to urban areas in search of work.
    - Ⓐ surrender
    - Ⓑ migrate
    - Ⓒ accept
    - Ⓓ stay

4. We must prepare for the _____ storm before it's too late.
    - Ⓐ illuminating
    - Ⓑ mythical
    - Ⓒ infrasonic
    - Ⓓ impending

5. This evidence seems to have _____ to the case I'm investigating.
    - Ⓐ portrayal
    - Ⓑ stability
    - Ⓒ prospector
    - Ⓓ relevance

D **Choose the correct word to complete each sentence.**

1. You have to book tickets in _____. (advance / chance)
2. I'm going to pay by check. Who should I make it _____ to? (in / out)
3. Please _____ of all recyclables in the marked bins. (throw / dispose)
4. A lot of medical terms are _____ from Greek and Latin words. (derived / arrived)
5. She had to _____ on the role of mother to her siblings when her mother died.
   (make / take)

E **Choose the word or phrase that is closest in meaning to the underlined word.**

1. The first radio signal was <u>transmitted</u> over the Atlantic Ocean in 1901.
   (A) found   (B) detected   (C) observed   (D) sent

2. Let's <u>scatter</u> the seeds in the garden.
   (A) disperse   (B) plant   (C) collect   (D) employ

3. It was a long, arduous task, but <u>ultimately</u> she prevailed.
   (A) indisputably   (B) subsequently   (C) nutritionally   (D) eventually

4. The amount of computer work involved was <u>mind-boggling</u>.
   (A) calculated   (B) unbelievable   (C) limited   (D) necessary

5. The <u>shrill</u> cry woke us all up.
   (A) odd   (B) low   (C) piercing   (D) desperate

F **Choose the word that is the opposite of the underlined word.**

1. He was a <u>brutal</u> dictator.
   (A) wise   (B) popular   (C) mighty   (D) gentle

2. He is well-known for his <u>altruistic</u> deeds.
   (A) cowardly   (B) selfish   (C) astonishing   (D) considerate

3. These findings <u>contradict</u> our original hypothesis.
   (A) challenge   (B) evoke   (C) confirm   (D) assemble

Actual
Practice
Test

Listening Section Directions

This section measures your ability to understand conversations and lectures in English. You will listen to 1 conversation and 2 lectures. You will hear each conversation or lecture only one time. After each conversation or lecture, you will answer some questions about it. The questions typically ask about the main idea and supporting details. Some questions ask about a speaker's purpose or attitude. Answer the questions based on what is stated or implied by the speakers.

You may take notes while you listen. You may use your notes to help you answer the questions. Your notes will not be scored. If you need to change the volume while you listen, click on the Volume icon at the top of the screen.

In some questions, you will see this icon: 🎧 This means that you will hear, but not see part of the question. Some of the questions have special directions. These directions appear in a gray box on the screen.

Most questions are worth one point. If a question is worth more than one point, it will have special directions that indicate how many points you can receive.

You must answer each question. After you answer, click on **Next**. Then click on **OK** to confirm your answer and go on to the next question. After you click on **OK**, you cannot return to previous questions.

Actual Practice Test 01

Note-Taking

VOLUME 🔊　HELP ?　OK ✓　NEXT ▶

1. Why does the student go to see the professor?
   - (A) To get advice on seeking a job
   - (B) To discuss changing her major
   - (C) To learn how to write a resume
   - (D) To request a letter of recommendation

2. What does the professor think about biology-related work?
   - (A) It requires multilingual ability.
   - (B) It offers advantages to younger applicants.
   - (C) It pays more than business-related work.
   - (D) Its job opportunities are limited.

3. Which factor will help the student get a job?
   - (A) Her work experience
   - (B) Her age
   - (C) Her ability to speak French
   - (D) Her business major

4. What is the student likely to do next?
   - (A) Attend the professor's seminar
   - (B) Revise her resume
   - (C) Submit her application
   - (D) Sign up for a business class

Listen again to part of the conversation. Then answer the question.

5. What does the student imply when she says this: 🎧
   - (A) She doesn't want to apply for the job.
   - (B) She needs more time to prepare her resume.
   - (C) She forgot to bring her resume with her.
   - (D) She regrets that she didn't complete her resume.

PART C

ACTUAL PRACTICE TEST

Actual **Practice Test 02**

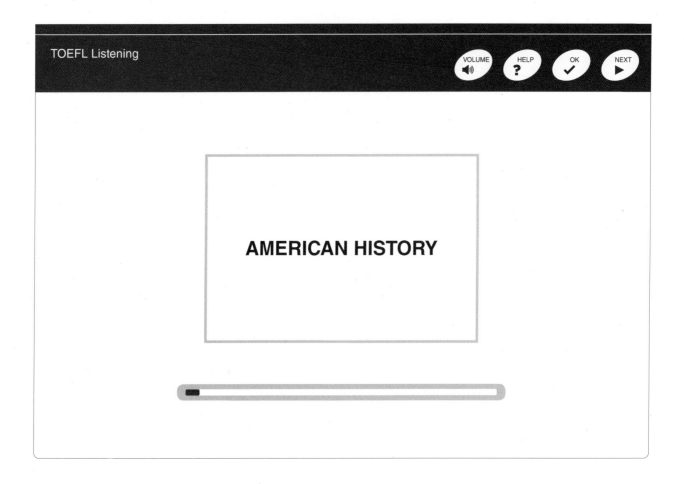

AMERICAN HISTORY

Note-Taking

6. What does the professor mainly discuss?

   Ⓐ The consequences of a legal decision involving GMOs

   Ⓑ The reasons why GMO research is perceived negatively

   Ⓒ Whether or not it is ethical to allow GMOs in our food

   Ⓓ How a GMO bacterium helped clean up marine oil spills

7. What does the professor say about GMO patents?

   Ⓐ They protect companies more than the inventors themselves.

   Ⓑ They encourage people to push forward with GMO research.

   Ⓒ They are having a negative effect on the war against hunger.

   Ⓓ They are no longer legal due to a US Supreme Court decision.

8. Why does the professor mention diabetes patients?

   Ⓐ To show how GMOs can adversely affect traditional medicine

   Ⓑ To give an example of a benefit of the Supreme Court decision

   Ⓒ To explain who opposed Chakrabarty's GMO bacterium patent

   Ⓓ To present a previous Supreme Court decision involving science

9. According to the professor, which of the following is NOT a concern of anti-GMO advocates?

   Ⓐ Harmful consequences to human health

   Ⓑ Potential damage to the environment

   Ⓒ A lack of information on food products

   Ⓓ The spread of oil spills in our oceans

Listen again to part of the lecture.
Then answer the question.

10. What does the professor imply when she says this: 🎧

   Ⓐ Chakrabarty's invention was brand new.

   Ⓑ Chakrabarty's invention was imperfect.

   Ⓒ Chakrabarty's invention was significant.

   Ⓓ Chakrabarty's invention didn't really exist.

Listen again to part of the lecture.
Then answer the question.

11. What does the professor mean when she says this: 🎧

   Ⓐ Courts might stop issuing GMO patents.

   Ⓑ Inventors might give up on their research.

   Ⓒ Consumers might begin to avoid GMO products.

   Ⓓ Companies might stop stealing the work of others.

Actual Practice Test 03

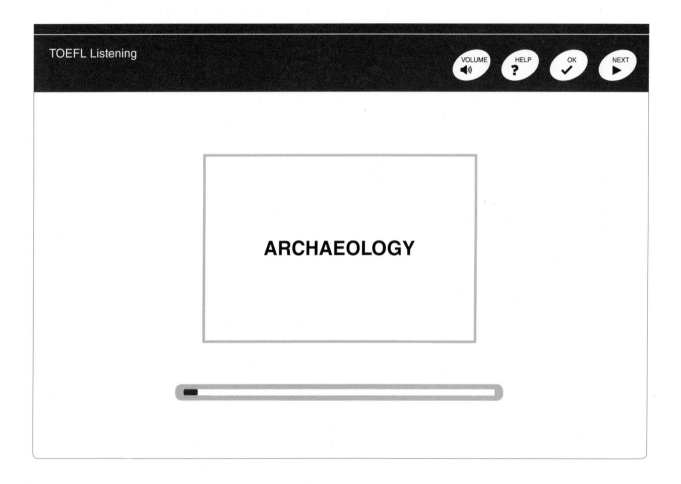

VOLUME

HELP

OK

NEXT

ARCHAEOLOGY

Note-Taking

VOLUME HELP OK NEXT

12. What does the professor mainly discuss?

Ⓐ The features of the Chauvet Cave paintings

Ⓑ Appreciation of the aesthetics of prehistoric art

Ⓒ The various ways of dating ancient artwork

Ⓓ The process of determining the age of the Chauvet Cave

13. What does the professor say about stratigraphic dating?

Ⓐ It is a form of absolute dating which provides a numerical age.

Ⓑ It is superior to seriation in determining how old an artifact is.

Ⓒ It compares materials of strata from two far-away locations.

Ⓓ It is based on sequences of strata accumulated in order.

14. Why does the professor mention Picasso and Michelangelo?

Ⓐ To emphasize that complicated design is much more difficult to create

Ⓑ To exemplify that art doesn't necessarily become more complex with time

Ⓒ To indicate stylistic changes between those artists can be measured by seriation

Ⓓ To demonstrate the application of dating methods to their works

15. What are the key features of carbon-14 mentioned in the lecture?

Click on 2 answers.

Ⓐ It determines the hardness of the material.

Ⓑ It decays at a constant rate.

Ⓒ It can be found in all organic matter.

Ⓓ It can be used as an accurate form of relative dating.

16. Indicate whether each of the following limitation belongs to stratigraphic dating, seriation, or carbon-14 dating.

Click in the correct box for each sentence.

	Stratigraphic dating	Seriation	Carbon-14 dating
Ⓐ A part or piece should be scratched.			
Ⓑ The development of art style isn't linear.			
Ⓒ It shows the age of material not the age of artwork.			
Ⓓ It indicates the minimum date of artwork.			

Listen again to part of the lecture.
Then answer the question.

17. What can be inferred about the professor?

Ⓐ He suggests that relative dating is no longer practiced.

Ⓑ He supports the point of view that relative dating is an unpopular method.

Ⓒ He points out the widespread use of relative dating in spite of its flaws.

Ⓓ He wants to contrast the uses of relative and absolute dating methods.

Actual
Practice
Test

Listening Section Directions

This section measures your ability to understand conversations and lectures in English. You will listen to 1 conversation and 2 lectures. You will hear each conversation or lecture only one time. After each conversation or lecture, you will answer some questions about it. The questions typically ask about the main idea and supporting details. Some questions ask about a speaker's purpose or attitude. Answer the questions based on what is stated or implied by the speakers.

You may take notes while you listen. You may use your notes to help you answer the questions. Your notes will not be scored. If you need to change the volume while you listen, click on the Volume icon at the top of the screen.

In some questions, you will see this icon: 🎧 This means that you will hear, but not see part of the question. Some of the questions have special directions. These directions appear in a gray box on the screen.

Most questions are worth one point. If a question is worth more than one point, it will have special directions that indicate how many points you can receive.

You must answer each question. After you answer, click on **Next**. Then click on **OK** to confirm your answer and go on to the next question. After you click on **OK**, you cannot return to previous questions.

Actual **Practice Test** 01

VOLUME HELP OK NEXT

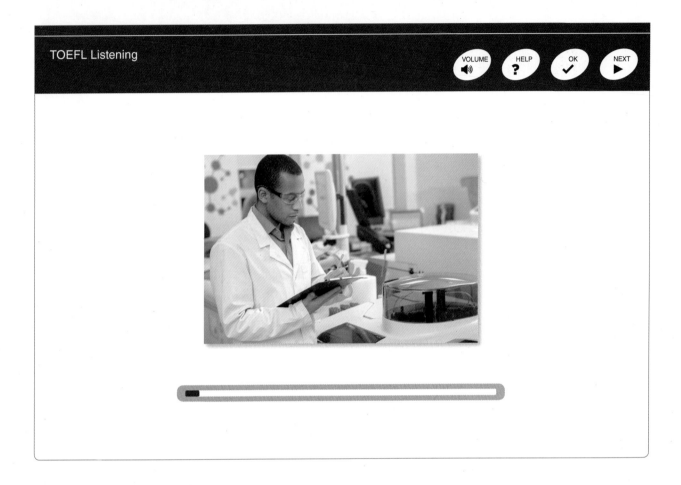

Note-Taking

VOLUME ◀))   HELP ?   OK ✓   NEXT ▶

1. What is the conversation mainly about?

  Ⓐ The benefits of taking lab courses

  Ⓑ Proper safety procedures in a lab

  Ⓒ How to launch a career in science

  Ⓓ The requirements of a lab course

2. Why does the lab instructor mention smartphones?

  Ⓐ To give an example of an item banned from the lab

  Ⓑ To suggest a possible method of timing experiments

  Ⓒ To explain why students must buy their own materials

  Ⓓ To emphasize the importance of accuracy in his course

3. Why is the student interested in the lab reports?

  Ⓐ Because she hopes they will facilitate her career goals

  Ⓑ Because she has taken similar lab courses in the past

  Ⓒ Because she is worried they will bring down her grade

  Ⓓ Because she wasn't required to write any in high school

4. What possible mistake related to purchasing items does the lab instructor mention?

  Ⓐ The student might buy too many things.

  Ⓑ The student might go to the school store.

  Ⓒ The student might spend too much money.

  Ⓓ The student might purchase the wrong items.

Listen again to part of the conversation. Then answer the question.

5. What can be inferred about the lab instructor?

  Ⓐ He aspires to having his work published in science journals.

  Ⓑ He believes that more work should be required of students.

  Ⓒ He doesn't care whether or not his students write lab reports.

  Ⓓ He feels that he doesn't have enough influence at the college.

Actual Practice Test 02

VOLUME   HELP   OK   NEXT

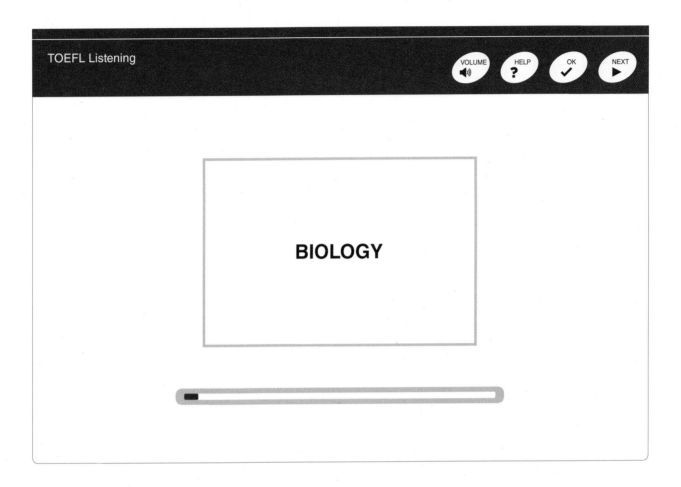

BIOLOGY

Note-Taking

6. What is the lecture mainly about?
   Ⓐ The biological prevalence of proteins in living organisms
   Ⓑ The function and acquisition of amino acids
   Ⓒ The difference between essential and nonessential amino acids
   Ⓓ The nutritional value of different types of foods

7. Why does the professor mention the alphabet?
   Ⓐ To explain how proteins were first discovered
   Ⓑ To illustrate how plant proteins are combined
   Ⓒ To demonstrate the difference between essential and nonessential amino acids
   Ⓓ To explain the relationship between amino acids and proteins

8. According to the professor, why are some kinds of amino acids called essential amino acids?
   Ⓐ Because they contain more nutrients than nonessential amino acids
   Ⓑ Because they must be obtained through food
   Ⓒ Because they are mostly found in plant sources
   Ⓓ Because they help out with the maintenance of the body

9. According to the professor, what are complete proteins?
   Ⓐ Amino acids that can be made by the body
   Ⓑ Foods that contain all twenty amino acids
   Ⓒ Foods with all nine essential amino acids
   Ⓓ Proteins made from a sequence of 3,000 amino acids

Listen again to part of the lecture.
Then answer the question.

10. Why does the professor say this:
    Ⓐ To confirm a surprising fact
    Ⓑ To correct an error in the lecture
    Ⓒ To clear up a general misconception
    Ⓓ To emphasize the main point of the lecture

Listen again to part of the lecture.
Then answer the question.

11. What does the professor mean when she says this: 🎧
    Ⓐ She does not plan to discuss the essential amino acids.
    Ⓑ She thinks the essential amino acids are commonly known.
    Ⓒ She does not want to cover a topic the students already know.
    Ⓓ She thinks the name "essential" is obvious.

PART C

ACTUAL PRACTICE TEST

Actual Practice Test 03

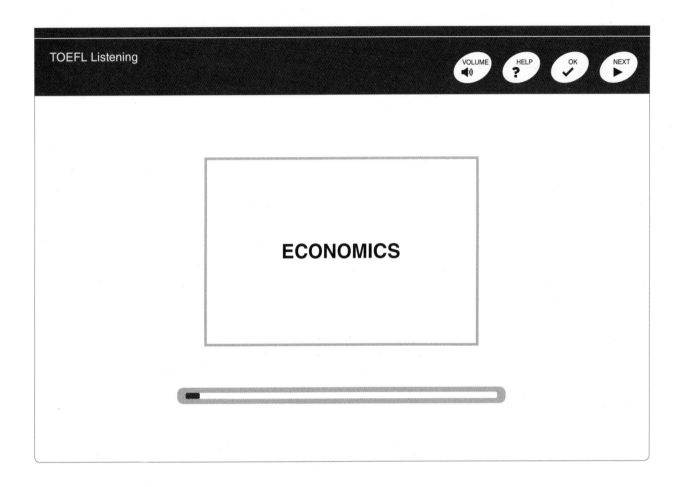

VOLUME

HELP

OK

NEXT

ECONOMICS

Note-Taking

12. What is the lecture mainly about?

Ⓐ A comparison of different types of businesses

Ⓑ How consumers affect the way sellers set prices

Ⓒ How businesses select a marketing strategy

Ⓓ An overview of several models of competition

13. Why does the professor mention the Big Mac and the Whopper?

Ⓐ To emphasize the similarities between products in monopolistic markets

Ⓑ To give an example of products in a monopolistic market

Ⓒ To illustrate the concept of product differentiation

Ⓓ To name two products that can be substituted for one another

14. What does the professor say about oligopoly?

Ⓐ It is caused by government control over public utilities.

Ⓑ It has a small number of sellers that are relatively large.

Ⓒ It is a model of competition that rarely occurs in the real world.

Ⓓ It has all of the same characteristics of a pure monopoly.

15. According to the professor, what are the factors that cause barriers to entry to form in pure monopoly?
Click on 2 answers.

Ⓐ A seller makes a product that has no exact substitute.

Ⓑ The government has licensed a company to be a monopoly.

Ⓒ A company holds the patent for a specific product.

Ⓓ People do not have information about every seller's prices.

Listen again to part of the lecture.
Then answer the question.

16. Why does the professor say this:

Ⓐ To introduce an explanation of a term

Ⓑ To get help with an idea he is not sure about

Ⓒ To find out whether the students are familiar with a concept

Ⓓ To indicate that a concept he mentioned is difficult to explain

17. What does the professor imply when he says this:

Ⓐ The students should already know some examples of perfect competition.

Ⓑ Most markets prefer other competitive models to perfect competition.

Ⓒ He cannot remember which kinds of markets demonstrate perfect competition.

Ⓓ Perfect competition does not actually exist in real life.

Actual
Practice
Test

Listening Section Directions

This section measures your ability to understand conversations and lectures in English. You will listen to 1 conversation and 2 lectures. You will hear each conversation or lecture only one time. After each conversation or lecture, you will answer some questions about it. The questions typically ask about the main idea and supporting details. Some questions ask about a speaker's purpose or attitude. Answer the questions based on what is stated or implied by the speakers.

You may take notes while you listen. You may use your notes to help you answer the questions. Your notes will not be scored. If you need to change the volume while you listen, click on the Volume icon at the top of the screen.

In some questions, you will see this icon: 🎧 This means that you will hear, but not see part of the question. Some of the questions have special directions. These directions appear in a gray box on the screen.

Most questions are worth one point. If a question is worth more than one point, it will have special directions that indicate how many points you can receive.

You must answer each question. After you answer, click on **Next**. Then click on **OK** to confirm your answer and go on to the next question. After you click on **OK**, you cannot return to previous questions.

Actual Practice Test 01

VOLUME
HELP ?
OK ✓
NEXT ▶

Note-Taking

VOLUME 🔊 HELP ? OK ✓ NEXT ▶

PART C

ACTUAL PRACTICE TEST

1. Why does the student go to see his professor?
   - Ⓐ To explain why he wasn't in class
   - Ⓑ To inquire about the poor grade on his paper
   - Ⓒ To ask for an explanation of his assignment
   - Ⓓ To ask about recruiting child subjects for an experiment

2. Why does the professor mention about her daughter?
   - Ⓐ To introduce a child subject for the student's research project
   - Ⓑ To emphasize the importance of proper predictions in the observation
   - Ⓒ To demonstrate the theory of children's cognitive developments
   - Ⓓ To facilitate the student's understanding about the assignment

3. Which of the following is NOT part of the project?
   - Ⓐ Observing a child's behavior
   - Ⓑ Interviewing a child
   - Ⓒ Reviewing the literature
   - Ⓓ Making a hypothesis

4. Why is the student supposed to meet an assistant in the Education Department?
   - Ⓐ To get additional materials for the project
   - Ⓑ To get information on the assignment
   - Ⓒ To set up an observation with a subject
   - Ⓓ To switch majors from psychology to education

Listen again to part of the conversation. Then answer the question.

5. Why does the professor say this:
   - Ⓐ To let the student know he misunderstands the assignment
   - Ⓑ To answer the student's question as to why he got a poor grade
   - Ⓒ To criticize the student's plan for conducting research
   - Ⓓ To prevent the student from leaving before getting a full explanation

169

Actual **Practice Test 02**

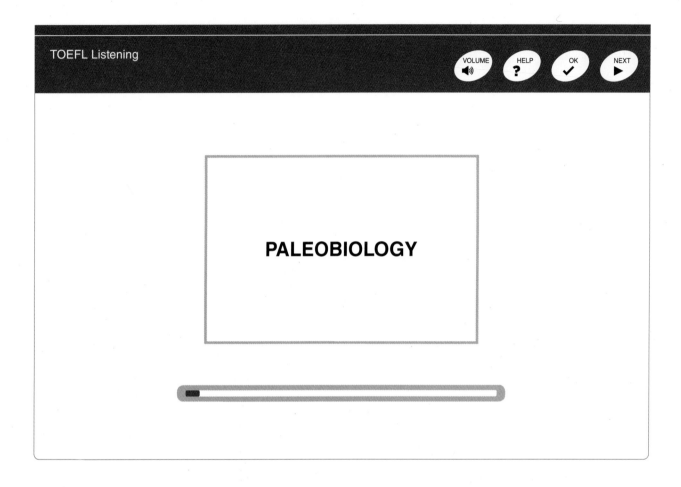

VOLUME HELP OK NEXT

PALEOBIOLOGY

Note-Taking

VOLUME HELP OK NEXT

6. What is the lecture mainly about?

　Ⓐ A possible reason for the large size of Paleozoic insects

　Ⓑ The ways various types of organisms breathe

　Ⓒ Differences between insects of the Paleozoic Era and modern insects

　Ⓓ The oxygen requirements of different types of insects

7. Why does the professor mention tabloid headlines?

　Ⓐ To emphasize that few people are aware of the size of ancient insects

　Ⓑ To give an example of a common misconception about insects

　Ⓒ To suggest how insect fossils were first discovered

　Ⓓ To introduce the idea that insects were once very large

8. What does the professor say about the Paleozoic Era?

　Ⓐ Air density gradually decreased.

　Ⓑ Oxygen concentration was higher than now.

　Ⓒ Most insects evolved during the Paleozoic Era.

　Ⓓ The way insects breathe was different from now.

9. What is the evidence for Paleozoic insects' size being related to oxygen content in the air?

　Ⓐ Modern insects have longer tracheae than the tracheae found in the fossils of Paleozoic insects.

　Ⓑ Small modern insects thrive in low-oxygen environments while large modern insects do not.

　Ⓒ Air circulation can be shown to correspond with the appearance and evolution of insects.

　Ⓓ Analysis of modern insects has revealed that larger insects typically have longer tracheae than smaller insects.

10. What can be inferred about giant Paleozoic insects?

　Ⓐ They might have survived because they had long tracheae.

　Ⓑ They were able to live underwater with their unique respiratory organs.

　Ⓒ They can't survive now because of the different level of oxygen.

　Ⓓ They became extinct since they couldn't move as fast as smaller insects could.

Listen again to part of the lecture.
Then answer the question.

11. What does the professor imply when he says this: 🎧

　Ⓐ The topic is somewhat unfamiliar to him.

　Ⓑ The students will have to study the material on their own.

　Ⓒ The students should already be familiar with the information.

　Ⓓ The last point is not particularly relevant to the lecture.

Actual **Practice Test** 03

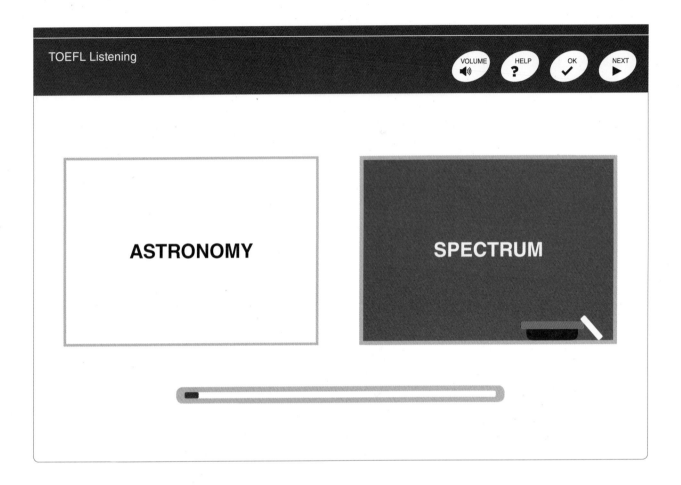

ASTRONOMY

SPECTRUM

Note-Taking

12. What is the lecture mainly about?

   Ⓐ The usefulness of spectra to astronomers

   Ⓑ A method for obtaining information about stars

   Ⓒ The nature and applications of spectra

   Ⓓ The proper understanding of radiation

13. Why does the professor mention absorption lines in violet, cyan, and red wavelengths?

   Ⓐ To give an example of radiation in the electromagnetic spectrum

   Ⓑ To illustrate that absorption lines are unique to each atom

   Ⓒ To explain how helium absorption lines would have looked to Lockyer and Janssen

   Ⓓ To name some wavelengths included in the visible spectrum

14. According to the professor, what can astronomers know about stars by observing their spectra?

   Ⓐ The types of radiation they emit

   Ⓑ The temperature of their cores

   Ⓒ The density of the gases in their outer layers

   Ⓓ The elements that make up their compositions

15. According to the professor, what resulted from analysis of the Sun's spectrum?

   Ⓐ The identification of absorption lines

   Ⓑ The discovery of a previously unknown element

   Ⓒ The realization that helium is incredibly abundant

   Ⓓ The determination that absorption lines are specific to each element

Listen again to part of the lecture.
Then answer the question.

16. What does the professor imply when she says this: 🎧

   Ⓐ The rainbow created by a prism is a spectrum.

   Ⓑ Spectra are not visible to the unaided eye.

   Ⓒ Spectra are relatively rare phenomena.

   Ⓓ The Sun's spectrum has a variety of uses.

Listen again to part of the lecture.
Then answer the question.

17. What does the professor mean when she says this: 🎧

   Ⓐ She wants to give only a brief explanation of radiation.

   Ⓑ She thinks the term "ionizing radiation" may be familiar to the student.

   Ⓒ She wants the student to choose his words more carefully.

   Ⓓ She thinks the student is using "radiation" to mean "ionizing radiation."

Answer Keys
& Audio Scripts

UNIT 01 Main Idea

NOTE

Highlighting and bold types respectively indicate the first and second repeated part in Replay Questions.

Underlined phrases show the answers of Dictation in Listening Practice.

Basic Drills p. 13

1. Ⓑ   2. Ⓑ   3. Ⓐ

1.

Listen to part of a lecture in a zoology class.

Professor: Anyway, it has long been established that wolves live and hunt in hierarchically structured packs. Similar to the way that... say uhm... birds have a structured social group, wolves also live within a "pecking order" system. At the top of any wolf hierarchy are the senior... or alpha males, presiding over the pack and showing their dominance in all matters of privilege and leadership. They also act as pack guardians – protecting the pack from strange wolves and other dangers. Below them there're as many as three other distinct subgroups. The alpha males' immediate subordinates are the other mature wolves, whose position is determined by age and physical ability. Immature wolves then follow, and they will not be treated as adults until they are at least 2 years old. Finally, the outsiders of the group, the erm... the outcast wolves are individuals cast out by the other members. Each individual wolf occupies a specific position within these subgroups. Higher ranking wolves take precedence over wolves of lower rank when selecting food, mates, or resting places.

2.

Listen to part of a lecture in a geology class.

Professor: So, understanding the causes that lie behind most earthquakes really took off around the 1960s with the development of the theory of plate tectonics. According to this... uhm... theory, the outer layer of the Earth is broken up into about 10 plates, 10 giant slabs of shifting earth. Imagine cracking a hard-boiled egg so that the shell is cracked into a number of pieces. Now in the case of the Earth, these pieces... or rather plates, actually float on a semi-molten material known as mantle, which is something like lava. As these plates float... they move closer to or further apart from each other, pushed along by the movement of the mantle. Sporadically, they get close enough to touch and stick together. The... uhm... the resulting stress gradually builds up on the plate boundaries and eventually becomes so great that the plates er... the plates rapidly slide past each other, releasing energy that has been built up for hundreds or thousands of years. This is what we feel as an earthquake. The colliding plates can cause so much energy to be released that they sometimes bring about another earthquake.

3.

Listen to part of a lecture in a sociology class.

Professor: So, social distancing... It's a new concept, right? Well, it may seem that way, but it's really not. It was actually discussed at length in the writings of Edward T. Hall. He was an American anthropologist active from the 1930s to the 1990s. Hall was very interested in how cultures differ from one another, especially in how they established and defined their public and personal spaces. This is where the concept of social distancing came up, although Hall didn't use that term. He did, however, coin a term for the study of how people deal with the spaces between one another. He called it, um, proxemics. Hall was especially interested in the amount of personal space Americans require to feel comfortable. Specifically, he studied why the amount was far greater than that required by Europeans. This need for more space, according to Hall, is a fundamental part of the American psyche. He believed it could be directly linked to many of the traits and behaviors associated with Americans. This idea holds true if we apply it to the 2020 coronavirus pandemic. While many Americans resisted certain anti-virus measures, most readily accepted social distancing.

176

Dictation

p. 14

1. wolves live and hunt in hierarchically structured packs   2. showing their dominance in all matters of privilege and leadership   3. whose position is determined by age and physical ability   4. treated as adults until they are at least 2 years old
5. understanding the causes that lie behind most earthquakes really took off   6. the shell is cracked into a number of pieces   7. the resulting stress gradually builds up / rapidly slide past each other
8. they sometimes bring about another earthquake
9. was actually discussed at length   10. was very interested in how cultures differ from one another
11. coin a term for the study of how people deal with   12. could be directly linked to many of the traits

Listening Practice 01

p. 15

1. Ⓓ   2. Ⓑ, Ⓒ, Ⓔ   3. Ⓐ

Listen to a conversation between a student and a professor.

Student: *[knocking]* Are you busy right now?

Professor: No, not at all. Come on in.

S: I was wondering if you had a chance to look at my story yet.

P: Yes, I did. You've got some great ideas. You presented a well-developed plot and used a unique style of writing.

S: Thanks. Do you have any suggestions?

P: Oh yes... yes. This is a good first draft, but you've got a ways to go.

S: Okay... what exactly were the problems you think I should work on?

P: Well, take the conversation between Ned and Rebecca. It doesn't really seem like a conversation at all, does it? Let me see... Okay, here... Ned just goes on and on and Rebecca doesn't say a word. In real life, Rebecca would be interjecting comments into the conversation, don't you think?

S: Yeah, I see what you mean. Actually I paid too much attention to showing the character of Ned. That's why I... well anyway... I can work in a few interjections.

P: Good. Secondly, a well-written story lets the reader make their own observations about characters. You have the narrator tell in detail what each character is like.

S: I thought you said characterization was one of the most important things.

P: It is... but don't be so direct about it. Let your characters' personalities make themselves known through their behavior. You need to respect your readers... they can figure out the motivations of the characters without you telling them.

S: Okay. I misunderstood the notion of characterization...

P: One more thing. You've got a lot of redundancies in here. Look here, you said that Ned was yelling loudly. *[laughing]* Have you ever heard anyone yell softly? By definition, yelling is loud. Then you've got Rebecca pointing to the "long-necked giraffe" at the zoo. All giraffes have long necks. So, you don't need to use those unnecessary adjectives and adverbs, which sort of umm... reduce the tension of your story.

S: Yes, you're right. Q3 *[discouraged]* Hmm... I guess I have a lot of work to do.

P: Well... **as a writer, most of the work that you do will be in revising. There is always room for improvement.** I look forward to your second draft.

S: Thanks for the advice.

P: That's what I'm here for.

Listening Practice 02

p. 17

1. Ⓒ   2. Ⓑ   3. Ⓐ, Ⓒ

Listen to part of a lecture in a history class.

Professor: All right. So the Plague, or Black Death, killed an estimated one-third of Europe's population during the 13th and 14th centuries. The epidemic brought an enormous amount of tragedy to the continent. However, this tragedy resulted in some good. One of the most immediate benefits was reform of the medical profession.

First... umm... medieval medicine may have been a catastrophic failure in combating the Black Death, but the consequences of its ineptitude were immediate and far-reaching. Both, uh... both physicians and scientists alike recognized the importance of medical advancement in order to fight disease and enhance understanding of human physiology. Back then, medical learning was based on the texts of the Ancient Greek physicians Hippocrates and Galen... written in Latin. In the wake of the Plague, the uh... physicians realized the shortcomings of these teachings, which were based on animal autopsies and were over a thousand years old, and sought new medical beliefs. Arguably the most significant breakthrough was the introduction of research based around the dissection of human cadavers. The church had previously forbidden the mutilation of dead bodies, as it believed that a soul would never reach heaven if the body were dismembered. However, exceptions were made, and by 1380, physicians' knowledge of anatomy was fairly accurate. This new focus on scientific theories and analyses became the basis of all medicine to come.

Uhm... in addition, the appearance of medical books written in everyday language is worth discussing.

Student: You mean they were written in everyday English?

P: Absolutely! As I told you just before, at that time most medical books were written in Latin.

S: So what did it have to do with medical reform?

P: As you can guess, many doctors... umm... including university professors died or simply fled during the Plague because they felt at risk from the disease. Such a chronic lack of trained physicians caused ordinary people to acquire medical guides and take command of their own health. But with... uh... high rates of illiteracy in Latin there were few who could read medical texts. Thus, medical books began to be published in English, providing them with more accessible medical knowledge.

Listening Practice 03
p. 19

1. Ⓑ   2. Ⓑ, Ⓒ, Ⓔ   3. Ⓒ

Listen to part of a lecture in a sports class.

Professor: Now, class, whenever we talk about a sports team or individual athlete, um... they all have one thing in common. That is, they all have a coach. And, uh, it's easy to maintain that the coach is the most important person to that team or athlete. Do you agree with that?

Student 1: I don't know, professor. I mean, it really comes down to the skill of the athletes to determine whether a team wins or loses. Sure, the coach can implement some strategies and impart knowledge about the sport, but...

P: Hold on there. I think you just pinpointed the big misconception most people have about coaches. You see, coaches have to do much more than give directions to athletes about their sport. Much more. Besides instructing athletes, successful coaches have to be able to demonstrate the skills they're teaching. They have to be counselors and motivators to their athletes... um, handling players' emotions and keeping the enthusiasm level high. And actually, there was a recent survey showing that the majority of coaches feel one of the most trying parts of their job is, uh, the organizational and administrative aspects of managing athletes.

S1: You're saying that coaches have administrative duties?

P: You bet. Administrative duties are paramount. They have to arrange transportation, lodging, and meals for extended trips... um, they have to find appropriate competitions for their teams to participate in. And let's not forget managing the budget for doing all this.

Student 2: Professor? This might be off-topic, but... I've volunteered to work at Dawson Elementary as a coach this summer.

P: That's great! What sport are you coaching?

S2: Soccer. And, well... I've played soccer before, but I've never coached it. Do you have any advice for me?

P: Sure. I was just talking about the administrative duties of a coach. Q3 🎧 Most students who want to become coaches take sports management courses here at the university. But I'd recommend taking a business management course instead. That'll really help you understand the administrative aspects of coaching. **Oh, wait... you said you're coaching this summer, so... that won't work for this situation.** But bear that in mind for the future.

S2: Okay, I will. Thanks.

iBT Practice 01
pp. 21-22

1. Ⓑ   2. Ⓐ   3. Ⓒ   4. Ⓒ   5. Ⓑ

Note-Taking

Your report is good → gave you an A
But you hardly open your mouth in class... why?
- not used to this kind of class (seminar)
- chemistry major → used to objectivity

Take part in the discussion!
- grade depends on class participation
- more than subjective opinions: art history
  eg. Renaissance & Baroque art

Listen to a conversation between a student and a professor.

Student: [Knocking] Excuse me, Dr. Bateman?

Professor: Yes, come in.

S: My name is Mike Dawson... I'm in your art history seminar.

P: Oh yes, have a seat, Mike. You must be here to pick up your report.

S: Uh, yeah, have you graded it yet?

P: Yes, I have it right here. [rummaging through papers] Q5 🎧 You did a great job, **actually... I was a little surprised...** here it is... I gave you an A.

S: You... uh... you were surprised?

P: Well, I really didn't know what to expect from you, Mike. You hardly open your mouth in class and I wasn't sure whether you had any interest in art history at all. But I can see from your paper that you have some keen insights. Why don't you share them with the class?

S: I don't know... I guess I'm just not used to this kind of class. I mean... I've never taken a seminar before. I prefer to listen to what everyone else has to say before I form an opinion myself.

P: I understand that, but you know, you don't have to commit to an opinion right away. It might help to hear how others in the class react to your thoughts.

S: It's just that... see, I'm a chemistry major. I'm used to objectivity, so I'm a little out of my element talking about art because it's so subjective.

P: Well, I applaud you for having the guts to step out of your comfort zone and trying something new. That's why I want to help you make the most of this class and honestly, the best way to benefit from this class is to take part in the discussions. That's why part of your grade depends on class participation. Of course... you can pass this class by writing superb papers like this one. But if you want to get an A, you have to take part in class. Class participation counts for ten percent of your grade, as you know. Now, you said you find it difficult because it's so subjective. But we do talk about more things in class than just our subjective opinions, don't we? It is art history, after all.

S: That's true. I guess I could think of it more like a history class than an art class.

P: Exactly. So, for example, what are the major differences between Renaissance art and Baroque art?

S: Uh... well Renaissance art, like the period, was all about human reason. Baroque art... well that concentrated more on human emotions and sensitivity.

P: Good, and how do these objectives present themselves in the actual artwork?

S: Well, Renaissance art is very symmetrical and... I don't know... it seems more organized than Baroque. Baroque is sort of all over the place... like... not so balanced.

P: See? Now you're talking art. It's not all opinion... you gave an objective description of each type of art to contrast the styles.

S: Yeah, I guess you're right.

P: Why don't you try starting by discussing objective points in class? Then, maybe when you get comfortable, you'll start sharing your opinions as well.

S: I'll try.

iBT Practice 02

1. Ⓓ   2. Ⓑ, Ⓒ   3. Ⓓ   4. Ⓐ, Ⓓ
5. Ⓑ   6. Ⓒ

Note-Taking

Intro_ Wetlands .
; periodically submerged in water, threatened by humans

Essential for many reasons
1. Great biodiversity
   provide food and place for species
2. Water quality protection
   remove nutrients and sediments that pollute water (like kidneys)
3. Flood control
   store water and release it slowly → decrease erosion

Change in attitude
⇒ conservation efforts seem to have positive impact

Listen to part of a lecture in an ecology class.

Professor: Wetlands are regions that are periodically submerged in water, whether it be by daily tides or seasonal flooding, creating an ecosystem that isn't quite dry land but isn't simply water either, such as a marsh, for example, or a bog or... an, um... an estuary. Q6 🎧 Like the rain forest, wetlands are threatened by the actions of humans. Many areas were either filled in with dry earth or flooded with water and converted into artificial lakes as they were thought to impede residential development and reduce the land available for agriculture. What we must recognize, however, is that this type of ecosystem isn't expendable... it's an essential component of our environment for many reasons.

These are areas of great biodiversity, the natural habitat of many species of fish and wildlife. Wetlands provide great volumes of food that attract many animal species. Organic material called "detritus" is formed when dead plant leaves and stems are broken down in the water. This enriched organic material can provide food for animals for part of or even their entire life cycles. Also, many bird species rely on wetlands for a place to rest during migration, to breed or feed, and to take cover from predators. More than one-third of all North American bird species are estimated to rely on wetlands for one of these purposes. In addition, in excess of one-third of all threatened or endangered species in the US either reside in wetland areas or depend on them. This is particularly notable given that wetlands make up only about 5 percent of the land area of the lower 48 United States.

Moving on, a major function of wetlands is water

quality protection. Although less well-known than its function as a provider of wildlife habitat, this role of wetlands is important to landowners and communities. Wetlands act like filters by removing nutrients and sediments that pollute surface and ground water. That's why they're often considered to be like kidneys. Both kidneys and wetlands, umm... help regulate water flow and cleanse the system. As the runoff water passes through, the wetlands retain excess nutrients and some pollutants, and reduce sediment as much as 85 percent primarily through the uptake of nutrients by plants.

Another way wetlands benefit humans is, um... well, it concerns floods. They work like a natural sponge, storing flood waters for a period of time before slowly releasing them, thus decreasing flood levels and protecting downstream property from damage. Wetlands also help to protect shorelines from erosion during flooding. This is because the root systems of wetland plants stabilize soil at the water's edge and help soil accumulation at the shoreline. Through lessening wave action and slowing current speeds, wetland vegetation along shorelines decreases erosion.

Now, as all these benefits of wetlands are explored, there's been some change in attitude: more focus has been put on preserving wetlands for their natural functions. Conservation efforts to protect these areas from development, as well as educational drives to promote understanding of both the environmental and economic value of wetlands, seem to be having a positive impact.

iBT Practice 03 pp. 25-26

1. Ⓒ   2. Ⓑ   3. Ⓓ   4. Ⓐ   5. Ⓒ   6. Ⓓ

Note-Taking

Intro_ Pollination
; the way seed plants reproduce → important

Parts involved in pollination
- pollen grains: male cells on stamen
- ovules: female cells in carpel (stigma on the end)

Ways of pollination
1. self-pollination: own pollen to fertilize, without outside help
2. self-pollenization: own pollen but need a pollinator
   cf. pollinator: moves pollen (eg. bee, wind)
3. cross-pollination: pollinator carries pollen to different plant

Differences in appearance of plants
1. by wind: large stigma, dull color, no scent
2. by biological pollinator: brighter color, stronger scent

Listen to part of a lecture in a biology class.

Professor: You've probably all studied pollination before in some of your previous biology or science classes... so today's lecture might be a review. But it's important information, so please pay attention. Okay. Pollination is... what? What's pollination?

Student: It's the way seed plants reproduce.

P: Good. And, obviously, pollination is important for plants because, without it, they wouldn't reproduce... and would eventually all die out. Now, let's look at the parts of the plant involved in pollination. First of all, there're pollen grains. Those are the male reproductive cells. They're on the male reproductive structure of the plant... called the stamen. The plant structure that contains the female reproductive cells – the ovules – is called the carpel. The carpel's basically the female reproductive organ. On the end of it is the stigma, which is the part of the plant that's designed to receive pollen grains. Do you follow me? [pause] Good. Moving on... there's a couple of different ways the process of pollination can happen. The first method I'd like to mention is known as self-pollination. This refers to plants that can use their own pollen to fertilize themselves. The male and female reproductive organs of a single plant come into contact with each other and pollination happens. Now, in self-pollination, this whole process happens without any outside help.

Okay, next I'd like to mention a similar process... um, self-pollenization. Like in self-pollination, in self-pollenization plants can use their own pollen for fertilization. But the difference is... in self-pollenization, plants need the help of a pollinator. Can someone define the term "pollinator"?

S: Yes. Um, a pollinator is something that moves pollen. Like a bee does.

P: Right. Pollinators can be biological, like the bee you mentioned. But they don't have to be living things. Take wind. It can transport pollen, right? So it's a pollinator. Pollinators are whatever moves pollen around. Got it? So, back to what I was saying, self-pollenization requires some outside help. From a pollinator.

And there's one more process of pollination that I'll mention. It's called cross-pollination. Q6  In cross-pollination, a pollinator... like wind or bees or bats or whatever... a pollinator carries pollen from one plant to a different plant. That's the key. *[slowly, to emphasize the point]* **The pollen comes from a different plant.**

Um, I'd also like to add that there're some differences in the appearance of plants that use biological pollinators and plants that use wind as a pollinator. Plants that're pollinated by wind usually have large stigmas to catch floating pollen grains. They're often dull in color and have no scent. And since they don't have to have insects land on them to deposit pollen, they don't need to have large petals. Plants that are pollinated by biological pollinators are quite different. See, they want to attract pollinators to them, so they usually have brighter colors and stronger scents. Um, here's an example. Flowers that're pollinated by bats are usually large, bell-shaped, and flashy. They're white or light in color and have strong scents. Also, they're open at night. As you can see, they're specially designed to attract their pollinators – bats.

Vocabulary Review   pp. 28-29

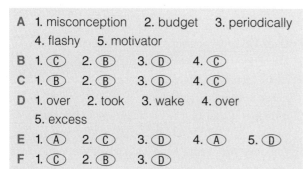

A 1. misconception   2. budget   3. periodically
4. flashy   5. motivator
B 1. ⓒ   2. Ⓑ   3. Ⓓ   4. ⓒ
C 1. Ⓑ   2. Ⓑ   3. Ⓓ   4. ⓒ
D 1. over   2. took   3. wake   4. over
5. excess
E 1. Ⓐ   2. ⓒ   3. Ⓓ   4. Ⓐ   5. Ⓓ
F 1. ⓒ   2. Ⓑ   3. Ⓓ

UNIT 02 Detail

Basic Drills   p. 33

1. ⓒ   2. Ⓐ   3. Ⓓ

1.

Listen to part of a lecture in a zoology class.

Professor: Okay. Courtship behavior, or courtship display, is the term for all behavior leading up to an actual mating. It is among the most varied and fascinating of all bird behaviors. The sequence and... erm... the variety of courtship behaviors vary widely among species, but they typically begin with territorial defense and song. Let's take the example of parakeets. It is the male who initiates the mating by going through his courtship display to the female. He... erm... the male sits close to his beloved and starts singing to her while puffing up the feathers on his head and throat. For brief intervals, he merrily dances away from and back to the female as he continues to sing. He repeats this routine several times, each time returning to gently tap her beak with his. Now the uh, the whole time this is going on, the pupils of the eyes are narrowed, and the feathers on his head and throat are still puffed up. If the female accepts the male's wooing, they have an actual mating.

2.

Listen to part of a lecture in an art class.

Professor: O'Keeffe has been a major figure in American art since the 1920s. Almost from the beginning, her work was distinguished from other artists' work in relation to the treatment of color, light, space, and natural forms. She mainly focused on simplifying and idealizing them. I mean... she was meticulous and steadfast in her devotion to synthesizing abstraction and representation. Understand?

Student: I'm sorry, but I don't exactly understand what you've just said, "synthesize abstraction and representation."

P: OK. I mean while her paintings often depict recognizable images and objects... umm... including such mundane subjects as flowers, rocks, shells, animal bones... they don't present those images in a very detailed or realistic way. Through her paintings, she reduces her subjects to the point where they seem detached from their actual form. The boundaries of her simplification of real-life objects stretch beyond convention, and her interpretations of them present fascinating independent observations. That's why her paintings are generally considered "semi-abstract."

3.

Listen to part of a lecture in a meteorology class.

Professor: One of the greatest dangers faced by drivers during winter is a phenomenon called black ice. Now, black ice isn't really black. It's actually transparent, which means the asphalt beneath it is visible. This makes the ice appear black. It is this, um, this transparency that makes black ice so dangerous. What happens is... well, basically roads become wet during the day. This can be from melting snow, rainfall or even condensation in the form of dew. When night falls and temperatures drop, a thin, transparent layer of ice forms over the road. This is black ice. To make matters worse, one of the most common places to find black ice is on bridges and overpasses. This is due to the fact that wind passing beneath these structures cools down the asphalt above and facilitates freezing. As black ice is effectively invisible, drivers tend to pass over it without slowing down. As their tires begin to lose traction, they slam on their brakes, losing control of their vehicles and, more often than not, becoming involved in an accident.

Dictation   p. 34

1. is the term for all behavior leading up to an actual mating 2. among the most varied and fascinating of all bird behaviors 3. they typically begin with territorial defense and song 4. It is the male who initiates the mating 5. returning to gently tap her beak with his 6. in her devotion to synthesizing abstraction and representation 7. they don't present those images in a very detailed or realistic way 8. to the point where they seem detached from their actual form 9. her interpretations of them present fascinating independent observations 10. One of the greatest dangers faced by drivers during winter 11. which means the asphalt beneath it is visible 12. one of the most common places to find black ice is 13. more often than not, becoming involved in an accident

Listening Practice 01   p. 35

1. Ⓑ   2. Ⓐ   3. Ⓒ

Listen to a conversation between a student and a professor.

Student: Excuse me, Dr. Reynolds, do you have a second?

Professor: Sure, what is it?

S: Well, I was wondering if I could reschedule my presentation.

P: Hmm... Why do you need to do that? Unless you really need to change it I want you to do it as scheduled.

S: I know... I'd like to present it as scheduled as well. But today I got news that my father is receiving an award on the same day I'm supposed to give my presentation. It would mean a lot to him if I could attend the ceremony. All of my family is supposed to be there.

P: Okay. When are you scheduled to present?

S: Next Friday.

P: Hmm... [suspicious] Do you want to do your presentation earlier or later than planned?

S: It doesn't matter to me. Whatever works for you is fine with me.

P: Oh, okay. [relieved] I'll see what the others in the class think. I'm sure it won't be difficult to find someone in the class who could use more time to prepare. If you wanted to go later, that might be a different story, but if you're prepared to go earlier, it should be fine.

S: Great. I appreciate that.

P: What does your father do, anyway?

S: He's a photographer.

P: Oh, so the award is for a photo?

S: No, it's actually for a book. He put together a book of essays on French novelists and their works and he included photos of them.

P: Oh, so your father is interested in literature too. What's his name?

S: Jason Tompkinson.

P: [surprisingly] Ah... really? I'm familiar with some of his photos... and I've heard about that book but I didn't realize Jason Tompkinson was behind it. Wow... what a unique idea. I love French literature. I must remember to pick up a copy of the book.

S: Oh, really? It's great to hear that. I think I can get you one. I'm sure my father would love to give a copy of his book to you.

P: That sounds great! [pleasantly] I didn't know I had the son of Jason Tompkinson in my class.

Listening Practice 02 p. 37

1. (A) 2. (D) 3. (B), (C)

Listen to part of a lecture in an entomology class.

Professor: Now, let's take a look at another type of social insect. The subterranean termite lives in large colonies with populations that can number in the, um... in the millions. Like other social insects, they have a caste system made up of workers, warriors, and breeders. Biologically speaking, termites are considered to be quite primitive. With the exception of breeding males and females, most termites are immature and underdeveloped... they are deaf and blind, and their bodies are soft and fragile, which makes them extremely sensitive to their environment.

Student: Excuse me, Professor. I'm just wondering... if termites are so delicate, how do they survive so well? I mean... it seems like they thrive everywhere.

P: Oh, that's just what I want to talk about today: how termites control their environment for survival. Well, as I said, termites are a fragile creature. They're especially susceptible to temperature and moisture levels. They require a warm environment, as they will not forage in extremes of hot or cold. When surface temperatures are unsuitable, they migrate deeper into the soil. And because their soft bodies don't retain water well and are vulnerable to drying out, termites require a ready supply of water to keep themselves hydrated. To achieve this, subterranean termites build their colonies in moist soil. For example, they are prevalent in sandy soils which contain more available moisture.

This is not all. Around their nest, termites build a hard wall made of soil, saliva and other bodily secretions, which not only protects the nest from predators, but also prevents moisture and heat from escaping. So, when the outside environment is unwelcoming, termites survive by controlling their nest. It's pretty impressive!

And when termites forage above ground, they have an even more, uh, ingenious method of avoiding hostile environments. If they find themselves needing to cross a dry, unwelcoming climate, they build shelter tubes or tunnels made from mud and other debris. These tubes, usually a fourth to one inch wide, serve as warm, dark, humid highways... the perfect conditions for a foraging termite.

Listening Practice 03 p. 39

1. (A) 2. (A), (C) 3. (B)

Listen to part of a lecture in a geology class.

Professor: The hardest known natural substance in the world is also one of the most valuable... and is considered by many to be one of the most beautiful. I'm talking, of course, about diamonds.

Now, one of the reasons why diamonds are so precious is that they are quite rare. And the reason they are so rare is that the conditions required to create a diamond are not only extreme, they are also quite specific, with little room for variation. Some sort of material containing carbon must be, um, exposed to an extremely high level of pressure, and this must take place in a low temperature environment. And please keep in mind, when we talk about temperature, low is a relative term. In this case, low is somewhere in the neighborhood of 1000 degrees celsius.

These specifics can only be met in two types of places. One is at the point of impact when a meteorite slams into the earth. The type of diamonds that are formed in these impact craters, however, are usually quite small and generally referred to as microdiamonds. The other location is in the earth's, um... lithospheric mantle. These regions are known as cratons, and they are found in the thick, stable sections of continental plates, about 150 to 200 kilometers beneath the earth's surface.

Now, any diamond that is formed in a craton is obviously going to be buried deep within the earth... and there it will remain, perhaps for billions of years, until something brings it up to the surface. So how does this happen? Well, one possibility is via an uncommon form of volcanic eruption that can take place deep inside of the earth. The magma involved in these eruptions is the, um... is the melted form of a kind of rock called kimberlite. When these eruptions occur, this molten kimberlite rushes to the earth's surface through tubular geological formations known as volcanic pipes, potentially snaring diamonds embedded in the mantle and carrying them upward. These diamonds are subsequently deposited in areas far closer to the surface of the earth.

iBT Practice 01

pp. 41-42

1. Ⓒ 2. Ⓓ 3. Ⓐ 4. Ⓓ 5. Ⓑ

Note-Taking

Purpose: want to switch majors
        (biology → literature)
→ big decision: why don't you take more classes?
- the longer, the harder
- parents like biology (high-paid job)
- but want to go grad & become a Hamlet specialist

How about dual degree? (≠ double major)
- effectively finish with 2 degrees
- doesn't take any longer to graduate
→ sounds perfect!

⇒ talk to your parents & see the academic counselor

Listen to a conversation between a student and a professor.

Professor: What can I do for you today?

Student: My name is Marissa Sanders. I'm in your Shakespeare class.

P: Yes, I recognize you from class. You sit in the front row. Your paper on *Hamlet* was excellent, by the way.

S: Thanks. I'm really enjoying your class.

P: I'm glad to hear it. What can I help you with?

S: Well, you see, Q5 🎧 I'm majoring in biology, but I'm enjoying this class so much... er... the Shakespeare class... well, I want to switch majors. I want to major in literature.

P: I see. I certainly appreciate your enthusiasm, but have you thought this through? It's a big decision. I mean, how many classes in literature have you taken?

S: I took Intro to World Literature first semester, and now I'm taking Shakespeare, as you know.

P: **Hmm... I don't want to let you down, but you know, one swallow does not make a summer.** Why don't you take more literature classes?

S: I know, but I'm going to be a sophomore next year. The longer I wait, the harder it will be to switch.

P: That's true... that's true. Uh... tell me, why did you choose to major in biology to begin with?

S: Well, I thought it would open a lot of doors. Plus, my parents were really pushing for me to study biology. They think I'll be guaranteed a high-paid job.

P: Have you told them you want to switch?

S: No, not yet. I think they'll probably try to talk me out of it. They'll say I won't be able to get a job when I graduate.

P: Is that a concern of yours?

S: Well, yeah, sort of. But I want to do something I love. I mean... I like biology, but I love literature. Writing a paper on *Hamlet*... and uh... I really enjoy analyzing Shakespeare's plots according to Michel Foucault's view. I even thought maybe I could go to grad school and become a *Hamlet* specialist.

P: Yes, you certainly have the ability. Have you thought about doing a dual degree?

S: Is that like a double major? I didn't think I could do a double major if one is an art and one is a science.

P: That's true, but you can do a dual degree. If you did that, you could effectively finish with two degrees. You, for example, would graduate with a Bachelor of Arts in Literature and a Bachelor of Science in Biology. That way you don't burn any bridges.

S: That would probably take a long time to do, though. I want to graduate in four years.

P: Oh, you can. It doesn't take any longer, actually, because all of your core classes are the same. And you don't need to take most electives if you do a dual degree.

S: Oh, I never thought of that. That would be perfect for me.

P: Why don't you talk to your parents about it, and then you can see the academic counselor for all of the necessary forms.

S: Great, thanks a lot.

P: I look forward to seeing you in more of my literature classes.

iBT Practice 02

pp. 43-44

1. Ⓓ 2. Ⓒ 3. Ⓐ 4. Ⓒ 5. Ⓑ 6. Ⓑ

Note-Taking

Intro_ Romantic Literature

against Classicism
- three unities: action, time, place (by Aristotle)
                strict Classical rules in European drama
                English didn't follow
  → limited human spirit → rebellion spread

Victor Hugo: leader of French Romantics
- his essay: demanded freedom from Classical conventions
- his play Hernani: disregard for three unities
  → battle of Hernani (audience fought)
  → defining moment in Romantic victory

Listen to part of a lecture in a literature class.

Professor: Q5 🎧 Who can tell me what a Romantic is?

Student 1: Well, um... since this is a literature class, I'm assuming you're talking about the Romantic movement of the nineteenth century.

P: Yes... it actually began in the late eighteenth century, but you're correct. What defined this movement?

Student 2: Weren't they trying to, uh, rebel against the old way of doing things? I mean… against Classicism.

P: Right. This was a primarily European movement that criticized the intellectual standards of the time, like reason, structure… the Classical school of thought. Now, when it comes to literature, there's a very good example of Classical convention – it's something we've discussed before… the three unities. Remember? Action, time, place… who came up with these unities?

S2: It was Aristotle, right? We talked about them when we covered Greek drama.

S1: Oh yeah. Aristotle said that drama should focus on one plot… and take place in one location and not skip around in time.

P: Good, you got it. And so, starting in the Middle Ages, the Europeans borrowed from Greek ideas like this and, um, sort of established them as hard-and-fast rules. So European drama through the eighteenth century stuck to the three unities.

S1: Wait a minute… we just studied Shakespeare, and his plays don't really follow the three unities.

P: Ah, sorry. I was too general when I said "European drama." You're absolutely right about Shakespeare, how his work contains multiple plots and jumps around in space and time. And actually, lots of English dramas didn't follow the Classical rules. But… just trust me when I say most European playwrights up to the nineteenth century knew there were certain rules they had to follow. Which brings me, finally, to the Romantics. How do you think the Romantics felt about the three unities?

S2: They probably didn't like them.

P: No, they didn't, and by the turn of the century, Romantic artists and philosophers were deliberately rebelling against Classicism. They felt that the, uh, strict Classical conventions limited the human spirit. This rebellion spread all over Europe, but I'd like to tell you about an important part of the story that took place in France.

In 1827, the playwright Victor Hugo wrote an essay that made him the leader of the French Romantics. He demanded freedom for writers from the traditional Classical structures, especially the three unities. Three years later, he wrote a play that embodied this freedom… and, well, it caused quite a stir.

The name of the play was *Hernani*. The story itself wasn't so revolutionary, but its passionate style and disregard for the three unities made it very controversial. Q6 🎧 On opening night in Paris, the audience was clearly divided into two groups – the young, enthusiastic Romantics, and the older, disapproving Classicists. Well, during and after the play that night, there was what's now known as "The Battle of Hernani." *[amusedly]* **That's right… this play caused a fight between the two groups… an actual physical fight.** It was quite an

exaggerated response thinking about it now. There were similar incidents during each performance of the play in Paris. But "The Battle of Hernani" was also intellectual… and it's seen as a defining moment in the defeat of Classicism by Romanticism.

iBT Practice 03

pp. 45-46

1. Ⓑ   2. Ⓓ   3. Ⓑ   4. Ⓐ   5. Ⓒ   6. Ⓒ

Note-Taking

Intro_ Locke's labor theory of property

Common belief: God gave Earth to share
⇔ private property
- individual is owner of his body and labor
→ land combined with labor belongs to him

Limits: too much property if it goes to waste
→ exchange? ok (with money)

Listen to part of a lecture in a political science class.

Professor: Okay, class. Today we're going to focus on John Locke. More specifically, we'll talk about his labor theory of property. I should first explain a core belief that inspired the labor theory of property. Q5 🎧 See, Locke – and many others – believed that God gave Earth to all of humankind. For everyone to share. **Okay. But, uh, wait a minute.** This belief about how God gave the world to humans to share conflicted with the plain and simple fact that people own private property. And owning private property takes away other humans' right – their God-given right, remember – to that property. So John Locke went to work to find a way to, um… justify private ownership of property… in a way that blended smoothly with the common belief that God made the world for all humans to share.

Okay. He started off by saying that there's a kind of property that only one person has a right to. An individual is the exclusive owner of his or her body. Plus their actions, thoughts, and beliefs. Absolutely no one else has a right to that property. Then Locke embellished upon this notion. He said that the labor done by a person's body and the work done by their hands also belong to that person. It's their property. And since that's the case, then if a person alters the natural state of a piece of land, they've combined that land with something they own – their labor. And by doing that, a person has made the land into private property. Q6 🎧 By performing labor on a piece of land, a person takes away the right of others to that piece of land. **So what constitutes labor?** Um, Locke defines labor pretty

185

broadly. It might be something as simple as picking up acorns from the ground. Or collecting apples. Or catching fish.

Okay. But Locke acknowledges that there should be some limits on ownership of private property. Um, one thing he stresses is that if a person has so much property that some of the goods on the property spoil before being used, then that person has too much property. More than their fair share. He pretty much says that as long as nothing goes to waste in a person's possession, then there's no problem.

There's actually a way around this, though. Say you harvested plums from your property, and you are unable to make use of the surplus before they spoil. Locke would say that if the plums spoil in your possession, you've got an unfair share of property. However, if you were to make an exchange with someone else and trade your extra plums for a product that wouldn't perish so quickly, that would be perfectly acceptable. You could trade your plums for nuts that would last all winter. Or, even better, you could trade your plums for something valuable that will never perish: money. So basically, Locke's saying it doesn't matter how much you own, as long as it isn't squandered in your possession.

Vocabulary Review   pp. 48-49

A 1. transparent   2. synthesize   3. depict
   4. squander   5. prevalent
B 1. Ⓓ   2. Ⓒ   3. Ⓑ   4. Ⓓ
C 1. Ⓐ   2. Ⓓ   3. Ⓒ   4. Ⓓ
D 1. into   2. neighborhood   3. down
   4. bridges   5. up
E 1. Ⓓ   2. Ⓐ   3. Ⓒ   4. Ⓑ   5. Ⓓ
F 1. Ⓒ   2. Ⓐ   3. Ⓑ

UNIT
03 **Function**

Basic Drills   p. 53

1. Ⓐ   2. Ⓓ   3. Ⓒ

1.

Listen to part of a lecture in a psychology class.

Professor: A number of studies are revealing fascinating insight into how color influences our emotions and... evokes specific responses. And this color psychology can be, or... rather is being applied to various designs of environment. Let's begin with an example of red. You may have noticed that you can often find red in restaurant decorating schemes. This is because warm colors like red, orange, and yellow usually stimulate the appetite. Meanwhile, blues are said to suppress the appetite. For this reason, weight loss plans suggest putting your food on a blue plate. **This is not all.** Blue also enhances productivity. Studies show weightlifters are able to handle heavier weights in blue gyms. Yellow is, er... usually considered an optimistic color, but... in fact, people lose their tempers more often in yellow rooms and... babies cry more frequently in yellow rooms. And the most romantic color, pink, is um... more tranquilizing. That's why this color is sometimes used to placate prisoners.

2.

Listen to part of a lecture in a chemistry class.

Professor: Activated carbon, also called activated charcoal, is treated with oxygen to open up millions of tiny pores between the carbon atoms and create an intensive surface area. Surprisingly, one cubic inch of activated carbon has a surface area equivalent to a 150,000-square-foot field. So, with the enormous surface area provided by its innumerable pores, a small amount of activated carbon can trap a large number of molecules, ions, and atoms. This process is what we call adsorption.

Student: You mean... activated carbon soaks up or, um... takes in things... like water or gas, right?

P: **Oh, well... that's absorption.** But, what I'm talking about is adsorption, which is, unlike absorption, the process of certain chemicals being attracted to something and then, bonding to it. That is... activated carbon collects substances on its surface. And because of this adsorptive capacity, activated carbon is recommended for air filtration of chemical fumes, gases, odors and so on. And the bigger the activated carbon, the more chemicals it adsorbs and the longer it keeps on working.

3.

Listen to part of a lecture in an art class.

Professor: Art Nouveau, evolving between the 1880s and 1910s, is an art movement that sought to dismantle the barriers... between the fine arts and applied arts. Now, according to Art Nouveau artists, an artist should work on everything from architecture to furniture design so that um... so that art would become incorporated into everyday life. According to their credo, the beauty and harmony of everyday life is improved by the work of artists, and their efforts ensure art's accessibility for everyone. Examples can be seen in a variety of paintings, architecture, furniture, glassware, graphic design, jewelry, pottery, and textiles. Even advertising posters have felt the effects of Art Nouveau. It was in sharp contrast with the long-held, um... customary distinctions between fine arts – painting and sculpture – and applied arts – ceramics, furniture, and other practical objects. So, Art Nouveau sought to redefine the essence and meaning of art... and to ensure that its obligation included, from that time on, any everyday object... no matter how utilitarian or mundane they might be. This was a completely new and revolutionary approach, **thus New Art – Art Nouveau in French**.

Dictation   p. 54

1. are revealing fascinating insight into / evokes specific responses   2. blues are said to suppress the appetite   3. suggest putting your food on a blue plate   4. more tranquilizing / used to placate prisoners   5. is treated with oxygen to open up millions of tiny pores   6. one cubic inch of activated carbon has a surface area equivalent to   7. being attracted to something and then, bonding to it   8. the more chemicals it adsorbs   9. so that art would become incorporated into everyday life   10. and their efforts ensure art's accessibility for everyone   11. It was in sharp contrast with / customary distinctions   12. sought to redefine / no matter how utilitarian or mundane they might be

Listening Practice 01   p. 55

1. Ⓑ   2. Ⓒ   3. Ⓐ

Listen to a conversation between a student and a professor.

Student: You wanted to see me?

Professor: Yes, come in. I have some good news. You've been nominated for a scholarship.

S: Really? What kind of scholarship?

P: It's a full scholarship to do your Master's in business administration.

S: A full scholarship! That's fantastic! Then I won't have to work part-time at the restaurant.

P: That's right. Your tuition will be paid for and you will also be paid for your work as a teacher's assistant. You'll get practice teaching and you'll learn a lot about researching. What do you think of that?

S: Wow... I think it sounds fantastic. Thanks.

P: Now, don't start celebrating yet. At this point you've been nominated within the department, but the final decision hasn't been made yet. I will say, though, that I think you have a pretty good chance.

S: What is it based on... like... what are the requirements?

P: Well, the first requirement, of course, is a nomination. That's taken care of... a letter is being sent to the dean on behalf of the department today. Second, you need to have good grades. You've got those. You're not having trouble in any classes, are you?

S: No, not at all.

P: Good. The last thing is your SOP.

S: SOP?

P: Statement of Purpose. You need to write a letter outlining your academic plan and what you plan to do after graduation. Basically, explain why you want to do graduate studies and what you plan to contribute to the field in the future.

S: Q3 🎧 Hmm... it sounds like a tough job.

P: Well, **think about the areas that you are passionate about and would like to explore**. What you need to do is convince them that it is in their interest to pay for your education. You do that by showing what you are going to do for the field.

S: Okay, I'll get started right away. By the way, when is it due? Could you look at it before I submit it?

P: Sure, I'd be happy to help. The deadline is March 4th, so be sure to bring it by my office at least a week ahead of time.

S: Okay, I will. Thank you so much.

Listening Practice 02 p. 57

1. Ⓐ   2. Ⓑ, Ⓒ   3. Ⓐ

Listen to part of a lecture in a medicine class.

Professor: Let's talk about COVID-19, the, um, coronavirus. I think it's safe to say that the coronavirus pandemic has been one of the most impactful events to occur in the 21st century so far. While this crisis has brought people together in many positive ways, it has also led to a lot of finger-pointing. There have been attempts to blame the outbreak on a wide range of things, one of which is globalization.

Student 1: Globalization? That doesn't make sense. How could globalization possibly cause an infectious virus?

Professor: Well, it's not being blamed for actually causing the virus itself. However, many people believe that globalization—or, more specifically, some of the things that globalization encourages, such as open borders, unrestricted international travel, and free trade—is what allowed the virus to spread throughout the world so quickly.

Student 2: So what do these people want? Isolationism? That might sound good, but I don't think most countries could survive being cut off from the rest of the world.

Professor: I think it's safe to say that you and I are on the same page. Other people are taking a more measured approach. They're calling for more international cooperation rather than more separation. Personally, I'm inclined to side with them. I simply don't see any evidence that globalization played a significant role in this situation. After all, there have been pandemics throughout history, some far deadlier than this one. Way back in the 14th century, for example, the Black Death managed to spread from East Asia to Europe, killing nearly 200 million people along the way.

Student 2: Well, there certainly wasn't much globalization going on in the 14th century, was there?

Professor: Exactly. There was not. So it's not logical to suggest that putting an end to globalization will make the world safer from infectious disease. And as for adopting a policy of isolationism, as you suggested, modern countries simply aren't equipped to go it alone. The end of globalization would likely mean the collapse of the global economy. Furthermore, it would make the, er, development and sharing of potentially important medical technology, such as new vaccines and innovative testing methods, harder to accomplish. Basically, in trying to avert a repeat of one type of disaster, the anti-globalists risk causing another.

Listening Practice 03 p. 59

1. Ⓓ   2. Ⓒ   3. Ⓑ

Listen to part of a lecture in an art class.

Professor: Today we're going to talk about Pop Art. This was an art movement that began in the UK back in the late 50s... but... well... it really came into its own in the US in the early 60s. Q3 🎧 But what is Pop Art exactly? We think of pop culture, also called popular culture, as kind of... kind of base... it's for the common people. But art... well, art is for the sophisticated... for the elite in society. **It is kind of a contradiction in terms, no**? Well, this elitist nature is just the kind of attitude that the Pop artists were against. They were opposed to the serious and highly personal movement of Abstract Expressionism that was dominant at that time. And... Pop Art blurred the borders between pop culture and art.

So, how did Pop artists try to eliminate the borders? Well, they did so by making art out of images taken from mass culture. Now, remember what was happening in the world at this time... this is post World War II, so America is seeing a huge economic boom. The message everywhere is "spend spend spend." People had more leisure time as well, and TV was huge. It was from this commercial society that Pop artists drew their materials. They often drew their subjects from television, comic books, movies and all forms of advertising. Subjects such as soup cans, comic strips, product packaging, celebrities, hamburgers, and road signs were popular.

At this point, I think I have to mention Andy Warhol. He is perhaps the best known artist of the genre. One of his paintings, named *100 Soup Cans*, is simply that... 100 Campbell's Soup Cans. Campbell's Soup, of course, is a major player in the soup industry and everyone was familiar with their labels. The soup can is an everyday item found in our consumer-driven society. But... Warhol turned it into art. Warhol and his fellow Pop artists were giving their commentary on contemporary society and culture, particularly consumerism, by using popular images and icons and redefining them. By doing this, the movement made art closer to everyday, contemporary life. It also contributed to decreasing the gap between "high art" and "low art" and eliminated the distinction between the commercial arts and the fine arts.

iBT Practice 01

1. Ⓒ   2. Ⓐ   3. Ⓑ   4. Ⓓ   5. Ⓑ

Note-Taking

Purpose: volunteer for campus excavation project

- Qualification? Take introductory archeology
- Now taking field techniques class → good chance
- Why campus was chosen as site? Farm community
  before
- Sounds interesting!
  → Position is not competitive
    Giving extra credit to volunteers because of a lot of
    work
- Schedule? Depends on how many apply
  → Will be informed of training schedule

Listen to a conversation between a student and a professor.

[knocking]

Professor: Come in. Are you looking for your essay?

Student: Uh, no, but...

P: Good, because it's not ready yet. What can I do for you?

S: I wanted to volunteer for the campus excavation project.

P: Oh good, good. I'm glad to hear it. Have a seat.

S: So, uh... what kind of qualifications do I need? I mean... is experience required? In fact, I've never done anything like this before.

P: That's not a problem. As long as you've taken an introductory class in archeology, you're good. And I know you have because you were in my class last year, weren't you?

S: Yes, I took introductory archeology from you last year, and this year I'm in your field techniques class.

P: Right. This will be a good chance for you to develop the skills you're learning about in class. I hope to see more students from that class apply. So, how are your other archeology classes going?

S: Great. I find archeology fascinating. That's why I've decided to apply for this project. Anyway, about the project... I kind of wonder why the campus was chosen as the excavation site.

P: Well, many years ago, before the university was established, this was a farming community. So there were a lot of farmhouses right here on campus. I think we'll find all kinds of artifacts – buttons, clay pottery... stuff like that.

S: Really? I wasn't aware of that. Q5 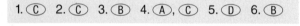 It sounds so interesting and I can't wait to get started... er... **if I get the position, I mean.**

P: Don't worry; it's not very competitive. And I appreciate your enthusiasm. You know, you're the first student to apply. I need five or six volunteers for this project.

S: I'm sure lots of students will be interested. They probably just haven't applied yet because they're busy with midterms or something.

P: I don't know... I'm thinking about giving extra credit to volunteers... you know... as extra incentive.

S: That's a great idea. You should have no problem getting volunteers if you do that.

P: Well, it's a lot of work... three or four hours a week. There ought to be something in it for volunteers, right? Anyway, I'm going to wait until Friday to see how many applicants we get.

S: So, what is the schedule going to be like, anyway?

P: Hmm... it really depends on how many volunteers we get. I tell you what, give me till Friday. I'll know then if we have all the volunteers we need. Then I will inform you of the fixed training schedule before we get started.

S: Training schedule?

P: Yes, even though you're taking the field techniques class, you still need training. We'll be dealing with delicate materials, so everyone has to know what they're doing. By then I'll know what the schedule for the actual project will be.

S: Great!

iBT Practice 02

pp. 63-64

1. Ⓒ   2. Ⓒ   3. Ⓑ   4. Ⓐ, Ⓒ   5. Ⓓ   6. Ⓑ

Note-Taking

Stringed instrument with a keyboard: piano

Before piano
- organ: keyboard, but wind instrument
- predecessors of piano
  ① clavichord (similar, but so quiet)
  ② harpsichord (not loud enough, low dynamic range)

Invention of piano
1. Name: pianoforte (means soft & loud) → piano
2. Advantage
   - could express much emotion
   - made composition simpler → great composers
⇒ a turning point in music history

Listen to part of a lecture in a music class.

Professor: Okay, I'm thinking of a stringed instrument with a keyboard. When the player hits a key, it causes a tiny hammer covered with felt to hit a string. The string vibrates and we hear a note. It's one of the most pleasant-sounding instruments of them all. I'm speaking, of course, of the piano. I'm sure you all are familiar with the piano.

The piano was not the first instrument to feature a keyboard. The first was the organ, but that's a wind instrument whose tone is produced by a vibrating column of air. The predecessors of the piano, then, which have both a keyboard and strings, were the clavichord and the harpsichord. The clavichord was first seen in the early 14th century and was pretty simple in design, and it was pretty small. It was essentially a rectangular box with a keyboard on the side. Of the early stringed keyboards, the clavichord was the most similar to the piano. Unfortunately, its sound was so quiet that you couldn't use it in concerts. It was usually played for small audiences of a few people in a small room. Then there was the harpsichord, which was a little more intricate in design... we won't get into the mechanics though. The harpsichord was louder than the clavichord, but not loud enough to be played for large numbers of people. Another disadvantage was... it had what we call a low "dynamic range." That means that the volume of the sound could not be altered by how hard you hit the keys. Q6 🎧 What the world needed was a keyboard instrument that could be played at a volume loud enough for concert halls and that also allowed expression through changes in volume.

That's why the piano had to be invented... so we could make these sounds for large groups of people. So, in 1709 a fellow by the name of Bartolomeo Cristofori invented the piano. He first called it a pianoforte, which means soft and loud. **Aptly named, don't you think?**

Anyway, the piano did what its predecessors could not do. First of all, um... with a piano, a hammer strikes the strings, and the weight and speed of the hammer decides how loud the sound is and the quality of its tone. So it made it possible to give a great deal of expression to the music... by being played both softly and loudly... and allowing the pianist to alternate between the two extremes. He or she could play gradually louder or... gradually softer. Through this dynamic range, they could express so much emotion. And... more importantly, the piano changed the way music was composed. Since its invention, it has become very popular as an aid to composing. The piano keyboard allows a composer to easily arrange the interplay of complex melodies and harmonies. So, composers wrote pieces just for one instrument, the piano, while they once had to write for several instruments. This change made composition far simpler. Thanks to the piano, many composers were able to make careers writing piano music and... over the past 300 years, many great composers have been known... as piano composers or virtuosos. As you can see, the invention of the piano was a turning point in music history. It's surely... one of the most, um, if not the most, important instruments.

iBT Practice 03

1. Ⓓ 2. Ⓓ 3. Ⓑ, Ⓓ 4. Ⓑ 5. Ⓒ 6. Ⓐ

Note-Taking

Eutrophication
- happens in water when nutrients increase
- good? water pollution

Cause
- originally natural process
- unnatural as a result of human activities
  eg. soil nutrients, fertilizers, sewage, nitrogen

Effect
- excessive plant growth: algal bloom
- block sunlight, deplete oxygen → death of fish
  → changes in species composition

How to prevent
- sewage treatment system
- buffer zones
- soil nitrogen testing (N-testing)
⇒ need to restore natural balance

Listen to part of a lecture in an environmental science class.

Professor: Eutrophication is a process that sometimes happens in sources of water. It happens when chemical nutrients in the system increase. Q6 🎧 Nutrients increase... so growth increases, too – **sounds like a good thing, doesn't it?** But, actually, eutrophication is a form of water pollution. Confused? Let me explain.

The chemical nutrients I'm talking about usually contain phosphorus or nitrogen. To some extent, eutrophication is a natural process, especially when the chemical nutrients come from natural sources. But the eutrophication that I'm talking about is the kind that's unnatural – that, um, results from pollutants that get into water systems as a result of human activities. For example, nutrients that we add to soil for agricultural purposes can get into surface water... and drain into lakes eventually. And there's also runoff from lawns and golf courses – places that use fertilizers. Sewage can cause an increase in nutrients in the water. Also, nitrogen that gets into air through the burning of fossil fuels can get into water sources through acid rain.

Anyway, when these nutrients get into water, they cause excessive plant growth. But, of course, not all plants are affected the same way. Certain aquatic vegetation grows especially fast... and basically chokes up the water source. One culprit is algae. Generally, they're too small to be seen by the naked eye. Um, but in huge numbers, they discolor the water... making it look green. There can be up to millions of cells per millimeter. We call this an algal bloom. Naturally, there's a, um, significant effect on the aquatic ecosystem when algae populations become extremely dense. Algal blooms block sunlight out from reaching organisms at the bottom of water. Sunlight is essential to all plants because it is used to produce energy and oxygen by photosynthesis. And, even worse, when large masses of algae die and decompose, they deplete the oxygen in the water. As a result, organisms, um, like fish and insects – they suffocate and decay. And the overall water quality decreases. The death of fish caused by algal blooms has another ecological effect, um... changes in species composition. That is, while most fish die from oxygen depletion, other fish that can survive in the new conditions replace the native fish. For instance, an increase in nitrogen might allow new, competitive species to invade and outcompete native species. They're different, and this change impacts the whole ecosystem.

Okay. So how do we prevent eutrophication? Well, basically, the attempt to reduce eutrophication begins with the sewage treatment system, even treating animal waste. And, making buffer zones is also recommended as a method of prevention. Buffer zones are, um, an interface between roads... or farms... and water sources for filtering pollutants. This helps prevent nutrients from draining into water sources. Another thing that's helpful is soil nitrogen testing. Sometimes it's referred to as "N-testing." See, farmers can test the soil... to reduce the amount of fertilizer they use. It helps them determine the minimum amount required. Which is great, because it helps keep the environment healthy, and it also saves farmers money on fertilizer.

As I said, algal blooms do occur naturally, but the effect of human activities has made eutrophication a big problem. Basically, we're looking for a way to restore the natural balance. Not to eliminate algal blooms entirely, but to make sure that they occur in more... natural patterns.

Vocabulary Review   pp. 68-69

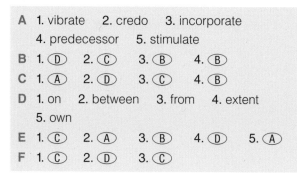

A 1. vibrate   2. credo   3. incorporate
   4. predecessor   5. stimulate
B 1. Ⓓ   2. Ⓒ   3. Ⓑ   4. Ⓑ
C 1. Ⓐ   2. Ⓓ   3. Ⓒ   4. Ⓑ
D 1. on   2. between   3. from   4. extent
   5. own
E 1. Ⓒ   2. Ⓐ   3. Ⓑ   4. Ⓓ   5. Ⓐ
F 1. Ⓒ   2. Ⓓ   3. Ⓒ

Basic Drills   p. 73

1. Ⓒ   2. Ⓓ   3. Ⓒ

1.

Listen to part of a lecture in an environmental studies class.

Professor: You're all familiar with the term "the grid," right? It just refers to the network of powerlines that are used to transmit electricity across a country or region. Today... Today we're going to talk about smart grids. Seems like everything is called "smart," these days, doesn't it? But in this case, I'd say it's an apt title. Smart grids make use of special meters installed in homes and businesses. These meters send vital information to a central computer system that, um, analyzes the data and uses it to make intelligent decisions about how much electricity needs to be generated at any given time.

Student: I'm sorry. I understand what you're saying, but I don't see how that's helpful.

Professor: Well, by anticipating peak usage hours, smart grids can prevent electricity shortages from occurring and keep prices relatively low by minimizing waste. And, um, that's... that's not all they can do. Smart grids also have the ability to integrate electricity generated by alternative sources, such as wind or water, into the main system. This ability will be crucial as we continue to seek ways to shift away from our dependency on fossil fuels and reduce emissions of harmful gases and other pollutants.

2.

Listen to part of a lecture in a marine ecology class.

Professor: An artificial reef is a man-made, underwater structure, basically built to provide a habitat for marine organisms. Artificial reefs, um... in theory, have two potentials: enhancing sport fishing by aggregating fish and, simultaneously, increasing fish stocks by providing more habitat for fish.

Student: Then, can reefs let us enjoy sport fishing without harming, um... I mean decreasing fish populations?

P: Well, if so, that would be great. Actually, artificial reefs have been shown to be highly successful for sport fishing because they attract fish, thus making them easier to catch. But, despite all the studies carried out on reefs for the past four decades, it is still debatable whether the reefs actually increase fish populations or... merely congregate fish.

S: What does that mean?

P: Well, if artificial reefs just attract fish and do not contribute to... as originally designed, to increasing fish populations, they may lead to the decline of fish stocks as more and more fish are caught.

3.

Listen to part of a lecture in a marketing class.

Professor: Green marketing is when a company communicates to the customers how green its products are. As environmental issues become the center of public attention, the trend is for more and more companies to jump on the green bandwagon. However, there's a common pitfall. Researchers indicate that uh... many green products have failed because the marketers focused on their "greenness" over... over the broader expectations of consumers. So, what does that mean? Well, the group of consumers with high environmental awareness is a niche in the market. Most, well uh... that is the vast majority of consumers are more likely to be attracted by a desirable benefit such as cost savings or improved product performance. Therefore, overemphasizing improved environmental quality of the product at the uh... at the expense of general customer satisfaction can consequently lead to failure in green marketing. Success in green marketing can be achieved when marketers fulfill consumer needs and interests as well as their obligations to protect the environment.

Dictation   p. 74

1. are used to transmit electricity across a country or region   2. make use of special meters installed   3. prevent electricity shortages from occurring and keep prices relatively low   4. have the ability to integrate electricity generated by alternative sources   5. basically built to provide a habitat for marine organisms   6. increasing fish stocks by providing more habitat for fish   7. have been shown to be highly successful for sport fishing   8. it is still debatable whether the reefs actually increase fish populations   9. how green its products are   10. center of public attention / jump on the green bandwagon   11. attracted by a desirable benefit such as cost savings

12. at the expense of general customer satisfaction can consequently lead to failure   13. when marketers fulfill consumer needs and interests

Listening Practice 01   p. 75

1. B   2. A   3. C

Listen to a conversation between a student and a professor.

Student: Professor Starr? Um... I have a favor to ask you.

Professor: Sure, Steven. What is it?

S: I'm applying for a job at Newton Laboratories. They're one of the biggest companies in the city and I'd really love to work for them. So, um... well, it would really mean a lot to me if you could write me a recommendation.

P: Of course I will. You've been an excellent student.

S: Thank you so much.

P: I have some acquaintances at Newton Laboratories and they're all very happy working there. Q3 🎧 However, competition for open positions can be pretty intense. They tend to favor applicants with more experience.

S: Yes, I've heard that. But I'm going to have a try. I've gained a lot of practical experience through working in the college lab, even though I have no working experience. It's worth a shot, I think.

P: Well, good for you. But... well, I'm curious why you've made this request to me rather than Dr. Grey. The two of you have collaborated on so many projects. I would think she'd have a lot of positive things to say about you.

S: Right, but Dr. Grey is away at a big conference in Paris. I heard that she won't be back until next week. And I have to submit my application by this Friday.

P: Well, as far as I know, she is coming back this week... umm... this Wednesday. I think you're mistaken.

S: [a bit embarrassed] Really? I must have got it wrong. But...

P: Well, how about this? I'll write you a recommendation, Steven, but I strongly suggest you ask Dr. Grey for one as well. As I'm sure you know, her recommendation would be more useful to you.

S: Oh, that's great. Thanks, Professor Starr.

Listing Practice 02 p. 77

1. (A)   2. (D)   3. (B)

Listen to part of a lecture in a botany class.

Professor: Take a look at this next photo. This is a rafflesia, the world's largest flower. It's a parasitic plant that's indigenous to Southeast Asian rain forests and uses only a few certain species of grapevines as its, um... host. Instead of performing photosynthesis, the rafflesia draws its nutrients directly from the host. The bizarre reddish flower of the rafflesia can grow to dimensions as large as a meter in diameter, even though its life span is only about a week. But even more extraordinary than the flower's appearance is its odor, which is most commonly compared to putrefying flesh. Who can conjecture what sort of purpose this smell might serve?

Student 1: Maybe it keeps plant-eating animals away...

P: That's a logical theory, but not the correct answer. **Q3** 🎧 Rather than attracting bees with the sweet smell of nectar, the rafflesia draws carrion flies with its stench and pollinates through them. The lured flies unwittingly spread pollen from flower to flower.

S1: How strange.

P: Strange is a very apt word to describe the rafflesia. In fact, scientists had to create a whole new family in order to classify the rafflesia, as it didn't seem to fit into any pre-existing category.

Student 2: Why? Because of its extraordinary size?

P: No, not exactly, but rather because it doesn't have leaves, roots, or a stem, which are... features typically used to identify and group plants. In addition, rafflesia lacks the genes most commonly used to trace plant ancestry, so even genetic techniques couldn't help. But... recent genetic analysis of the rafflesia's DNA determined that, um, it belongs to the same family as the rubber tree... despite the fact that all the other plants in this family have extremely small flowers.

S2: If so... how come only the rafflesia is so big?

P: Well, millions of years ago, the flowers of the rafflesia family were apparently only a couple of millimeters across... but a larger size provided a competitive advantage when attracting insects for pollination, allowing their odor to be more widely distributed and... making them easier to spot on the crowded floor of the rain forest. Consequently, they underwent rapid evolution... eventually achieving their current impressive size.

Listening Practice 03 p. 79

1. (D)   2. (A)   3. (D)

Listen to part of a lecture in a music class.

Professor: Continuing our lessons on jazz and contemporary music, I'd like to take a moment to touch upon a woman by the name of Regina Carter. And, I can... I can tell by the expressions on some of your faces that you're familiar with her work. Regina Carter is, of course, a modern jazz musician. A musical prodigy, she began playing the violin at the age of 4 with the intent of becoming a classical violinist, eventually switching to jazz while in college.

Now the reason I brought up Ms. Carter... is the, um, fact that due to her reputation as an outstanding jazz violinist, she was given one of the rarest opportunities in music – a chance to play the Cannon, the legendary hand-crafted violin, made in Italy more than 260 years ago. Now, the Cannon takes its name from its huge sonorous sound, and is not an instrument for the fainthearted. Way back in the 19th century it belonged to the great Paganini, arguably the most important violinist of all time, and since then... the uh... the proud citizens of Genoa, which is where the Cannon is kept, have allowed only a handful of people to play it. **Q3** 🎧 Okay, now getting back to Carter, um, some people feared a jazz musician wasn't worthy of such an honor, but the concert Carter played was a great success. In addition, she was given a chance to record her album with the Cannon. Well, she was the first non-classical musician to play the Cannon, as well as the first black person.

The reason it worked out so well, as well as the reason I brought up this anecdote, were the common traits shared by Regina Carter and Paganini... that is, in the variations and innovative techniques they used to play the violin. Classical baroque musicians such as Paganini often used improvisation, which is also, as you all know, a main feature of modern jazz musicians. So what I want to emphasize here is, although the music they play may sound different, jazz violinists and classical violinists are still very much part of the same manner and tradition.

iBT Practice 01

pp. 81-82

1. Ⓓ   2. Ⓓ   3. Ⓑ   4. Ⓒ   5. Ⓐ

Note-Taking

Why not extend your hours during exams?
  ① vending machines: only beverages
  ② convenience store: 20 min away
  ③ fast food restaurant: closes at 10, policies by head
    office
⇒ No, not feasible
  workers = students → will be short-staffed

A petition with over 1000 signatures → a lot of business
⇒ will open till 12 am

Listen to a conversation between a student and a snack bar manager.

Snack bar manager: What can I get for you?

Student: Actually, I'm not here to buy anything. I have a suggestion for you.

M: Oh? Okay, shoot.

S: I'm the president of the student council and live in the dorm now, and, well, as you probably know, we students are taking our exams next week.

M: Yes, I'm aware of that.

S: Well, don't you think it would be a good idea to extend your business hours during exams? A lot of students will be staying up late to study and there is nothing around that's open if we want a snack or a cup of coffee to keep us going. There're vending machines in the dorms, but they sell only a few beverages. If we want something substantial late at night, we have to walk for about twenty minutes to the nearest twenty-four-hour convenience store.

M: What about that fast food restaurant across the street? When do they close?

S: They close at ten o'clock. Actually, I just made the same suggestion over there. The manager said it was a good idea, but there was nothing she could do because it's a chain restaurant. They have to follow the policies laid out by head office, so they can't change the business hours arbitrarily.

M: I see. That makes sense.

S: But you're not a chain. As manager, you could change the store hours just for a week, couldn't you?

M: Well, I suppose, but it wouldn't be feasible to stay open twenty-four hours.

S: I'm not suggesting that. I was just thinking that if you stayed open till... say... one a.m. instead of closing at nine... that would be great for students needing a late night snack.

M: [skeptical] I don't know. What about the workers? They're students too, you know. They also need to study next week and I'll be short-staffed. Plus, I know the cleaning staff won't stay late. There would be an extra burden on the cashiers to take on the cleaning duties too.

S: Look. I have a petition here with over a thousand signatures on it. These are all students who would like the snack bar to stay open late at night. That's a thousand students wanting to make purchases at this snack bar late at night... that's a lot of business. You could afford to offer extra pay to anyone who volunteered to work the extra hours. I'm sure that would be very popular among your staff. As far as cleaning goes, you could make it "take-out only" late at night. Then there'd be less mess to clean up.

M: A thousand signatures, you say? That is a lot of business. I'll tell you what... we'll compromise. I'll stay open until twelve midnight. That's three hours longer than we normally stay open. I think you students can try to make it here before midnight, can't you?

S: Twelve midnight sounds great.

M: Okay, I'll have to run it by my staff first and make sure I'll be able to keep the place properly staffed. If it all works out I'll hang a poster on the door.

S: Wonderful! Thank you so much for listening.

M: Thank you for the suggestion.

iBT Practice 02

pp. 83-84

1. Ⓐ   2. Ⓓ   3. Ⓒ   4. Ⓑ   5. Ⓒ   6. Ⓓ

Note-Taking

Business metrics = measurements to analyze companies
  - used to determine KPIs

1. financial performance index (KPI) - company's financial
   situation
   - metrics → sales growth, net profit margin, cash flow

2. customer satisfaction (KPI) - as important as financial
   performance index
   - metrics → customer satisfaction surveys, customer
    retention rates

3. internal process quality (KPI) - day-to-day tasks
   - metrics → capacity utilization, project performance,
    product quality.

4. employee satisfaction (KPI) - most important factor in a
   successful business
   - metrics → employee engagement, absentee rates.

Used by:
  - companies, consultants, investors

Listen to part of a lecture in a business class.

Professor: Today I want to talk about business metrics and KPIs, specifically how they relate to one another. First off, business metrics... There's a term I'm sure you've heard fairly often, but you might not be sure exactly what it refers to. So here's a, um, a very basic definition. Business metrics are measurements that people use to analyze a company's performance and condition. **Q5**

🎧 In other words, metrics are basically just statistics, at least in and of themselves. But they're statistics that hold the key to some vital information. That's because we can use business metrics to determine a company's KPIs. This stands for key performance indicators.

There's, um, there's a variety of KPIs that exist. But today I want to talk to you about the four most important ones, at least in my opinion. So, let's get the ball rolling with something called the financial performance index. The financial performance index is simply the KPI that divulges information about a company's financial situation. Obviously, money is one of the most crucial factors to consider when it comes to the health of businesses. Some of the metrics we use to calculate the financial performance index include sales growth, net profit margin and cash flow.

The next one is customer satisfaction. To measure this KPI, you'll want to look at things like customer satisfaction surveys and customer retention rates. The latter essentially means what percentage of your customers are sticking around and what percentage are going elsewhere. Although it might not seem that way, this KPI is just as important as the financial performance index. After all, without customers, a business can't earn any money.

Number three on the KPI list is internal process quality. As the name clearly states, this analyzes the quality of the company's internal processes. You know, the, um, day-to-day tasks that keep a business running. What are some metrics that tell us about this? Well, there's capacity utilization, which basically measures whether or not a company is optimizing its resources. You'd also want to look at things like project performance and product quality.

Okay, so the final KPI I want to mention today involves another type of satisfaction... not customer satisfaction, but employee satisfaction. You might not think big companies care about their workers, but believe me, they do... Or at least they should. **Q6** 🎧 There's been a lot of talk about robots replacing human workers, but that's mostly just conjecture. Right now, happy, productive employees are the most important factor in a successful business, and it's likely to remain that way. The, er, the metrics that... that are used to measure employee satisfaction include employee engagement and absentee rates.

So... who exactly is using these KPIs to analyze companies? Well, it varies. Sometimes it's the company itself, trying, you know, to get a better handle on what it is doing right and what it is doing wrong. Or it could be an outside consultant who was hired to figure out ways to improve things. And, of course, potential investors are very interested in business metrics. They commonly want to see a company's KPIs before they start putting money into it.

iBT Practice 03

pp. 85-86

1. Ⓑ   2. Ⓓ   3. Light zone - Ⓑ, Ⓒ / Dark zone - Ⓐ / Neither - Ⓓ   4. Ⓐ, Ⓓ   5. Ⓐ
6. Ⓑ

Note-Taking

Moon: its geological aspects
; molted with patches (= zones)

2 types of zones
  ① dark zone: lunar maria (means sea → misnomer)
               formed by lava
  ② white zone: terra (means land → misnomer)
              higher altitude regions
              many craters caused by impacts of
              comets & asteroids
              ⇔ maria: few craters (because filled in
                by lava)

Why does the Moon have many craters unlike the Earth?
- thin atmosphere → allows many impacts
- no erosion → craters remain preserved

Listen to part of a lecture in an astronomy class.

Professor: Now, I'd like to talk a bit about the Moon... about some of its basic geological aspects. Even from the Earth, without the aid of a telescope, we can easily discern that the Moon is not in possession of a completely regular surface. Instead, it appears to be mottled with dark and light patches.

These patches are, um... they're what we call zones, areas with distinctly different geological characteristics. There are two types of zones, aptly named dark and light. The dark zones are known as "lunar maria." Maria is the Latin word for "seas." This is a misnomer that came about when ancient astronomers gazing at the Moon mistook these large areas for oceans. In actuality, they are plains, formed by the... the lava flow from volcanic eruptions billions of years ago.

195

The light zones are the highlands of the Moon. They are sometimes also referred to as "terra," Latin for land, as they were erroneously believed to be continents surrounded by water. These are higher altitude regions, much older than the maria, and they are riddled with craters. These craters were caused by the impact of comets and asteroids traveling through space at high velocities... which is why we call them impact craters. Such impacts have been occurring for eons and continue even today, although at a lesser rate. Across the entire surface of the Moon, there's estimated to be about half a million craters of significant size. By the way, there are few craters visible in the maria, the dark zones... that's because they have for the most part been filled in by molten lava that has since solidified.

Student: Q5 🎧 Excuse me, Professor? Why does the Moon have so many impact craters, but the Earth doesn't? **I mean, they're right next to each other.**

P: Good question. There are a couple of reasons. Q6 🎧 Um... what can you tell me about the Moon's atmosphere?

S: The Moon's atmosphere? Well... um, compared to the Earth, it, er... wait a minute, the Moon doesn't have an atmosphere.

P: That's right, it basically doesn't. The Moon's atmosphere is so thin as to be practically non-existent. And it's precisely this lack of an atmosphere that allows so many impacts to take place. Many of the comets and asteroids that would seem destined to strike the Earth burn up from friction as they pass through our atmosphere. And also, because there's, um, no atmosphere on the Moon, there's no rain or wind, which means there is very little erosion. Without erosion, geographical features remain unchanged for long periods of time, unlike the Earth where our landscapes are in a constant state of flux. Therefore, many of these craters on the Moon have remained well-preserved. There are impact craters to be found on the Earth, but having been eroded away, they are not nearly as prominent as those on the Moon.

Vocabulary Review   pp. 88-89

A 1. optimize   2. conjecture   3. analyze
   4. putrefy   5. simultaneously
B 1. Ⓒ   2. Ⓒ   3. Ⓑ   4. Ⓓ
C 1. Ⓒ   2. Ⓑ   3. Ⓒ   4. Ⓑ
D 1. expense   2. bandwagon   3. trace
   4. molten
E 1. Ⓓ   2. Ⓒ   3. Ⓐ   4. Ⓓ   5. Ⓑ
   6. Ⓑ
F 1. Ⓐ   2. Ⓓ   3. Ⓒ

UNIT

05 Organization

Basic Drills

p. 93

1. C   2. D   3. B

1.

Listen to part of a lecture in a linguistics class.

Professor: To converse efficiently, interlocutors have to respect the cooperative principles besides uh... language itself, like vocabulary or grammar. Professor Grice introduces four maxims for successful communication. Now let me explain the first of these: quantity. This is about... it's about saying what's required, no more or less than necessary information. Imagine that you are going to meet your friend at a museum. You've been waiting in front of the museum for a while, but he hasn't shown up. In fact, he's been waiting for you inside the building. So, what's the problem here? You didn't mention the exact place; in other words, you gave less information than required. However, had you told your friend to meet under the third window next to the second pillar, 5 feet away from the front gate of the museum, well, your friend would never hang out with you. So, more or less information than what is required in the conversation can uh... well it hinders the listener from inferring the real meaning of the utterance, and makes it impossible to have a truthful communication between participants.

2.

Listen to part of a lecture in a physics class.

Professor: According to Newton's first law of motion, inertia is the property of an object that remains constant in velocity unless acted upon by an outside force. In short, objects tend to keep on doing what they're doing. Actually, the... the dominant thought prior to Newton's day was that objects naturally came to a resting position. Moving objects, so it was believed, would uhm... eventually just stop moving. However, Newton's conception of inertia directly opposed this idea. He declared that an object wouldn't actually stop moving unless an opposite force on the object stops it. For instance, once we push a book on... let's say a tabletop, the book would continue moving with the same speed

and direction forever. But, old people thought that was ridiculous because this phenomenon doesn't... just doesn't actually happen in the real world. Why is that?

Student: Because there is friction on the table.

P: Excellent. The book in motion eventually comes to a resting position because of... well as you said, friction, and that is another force applied to the book. But again, without the force of friction, the sliding book would keep moving.

3.

Listen to part of a lecture in an entomology class.

Professor: Now... all insects grow through distinct stages, and we call this developmental transition metamorphosis. There are two types of metamorphosis – incomplete and complete. Okay, first of all I want to cover incomplete metamorphosis. Now this type of metamorphosis consists of 3 stages and about 12% of all insects go through egg, nymph, and adult transitions. First, during the egg stage, a female insect lays eggs. These eggs are often covered by an egg case, which protects the eggs and holds them together. Next, during the nymph stage, the eggs hatch into nymphs. Nymphs resemble adult insects, but usually don't have wings. They will also eat the same food that the adult insects eat. As they grow, nymphs shed or molt their exoskeletons, you know, outer casings made up of a hard substance called chitin... and replace them with larger ones. Before reaching maturity a nymph may molt between 4 and 8 times. Once the insect has developed into its full adult phase, it will cease to molt and will have grown wings.

Dictation

p. 94

1. To converse efficiently / respect the cooperative principles 2. no more or less than necessary information 3. hinders the listener from inferring the real meaning of the utterance 4. remains constant in velocity unless acted upon by an outside force 5. objects naturally came to a resting position 6. unless an opposite force on the object stops it 7. old people thought that was ridiculous 8. that is another force applied to the book 9. all insects grow through distinct stages 10. during the nymph stage, the eggs hatch into nymphs 11. resemble adult insects 12. outer casings made up of a hard substance 13. Once the insect has developed into its full adult phase

Listening Practice 01

1. D 2. C 3. Intrusive rocks - C /
Extrusive rocks - A, B

Listen to part of a lecture in an earth science class.

Professor: Today, we need to briefly cover the topic of igneous rocks. These are rocks that are formed from magma or lava. Magma is subterranean molten rock, um... deep within the earth's mantle or crust. When this magma spews forth onto the surface, say through a volcanic eruption... we refer to it as lava. The material remains unchanged, but now that it exists under a different set of circumstances, we refer to it by a different name. It's sort of like when a cloud descends to the ground, we no longer call it a cloud. It's now fog. Anyway... when this material cools down, it solidifies into igneous rock.

There are hundreds of kinds of igneous rocks, but they can all be classified into one of two broad categories, based on the circumstance of their formation. Intrusive rocks, such as granite, are formed beneath the earth from cooling magma, while extrusive rocks – for example, basalt – are formed on the earth's surface from cooling lava. For this reason, extrusive rock is commonly referred to as lava rock. And, among over 700 types of igneous rocks that have been described, most igneous rocks are intrusive rocks, formed beneath the surface of the earth's crust.

These rocks can be visually differentiated with the naked eye by breaking them open and observing the quality of their, um, grain. Because intrusive rocks crystallize slowly in the heat of the earth's crust or mantle, sometimes taking millions of years to harden, the result is a coarse grain. Extrusive rocks, on the other hand, crystallize quickly – in a matter of days, in fact – as the lava is exposed to the earth's cool surface. Because of this, a finer grain develops.

Now, although they are not particularly evident on the earth's surface, if you were to drill down a bit, you'd eventually see that igneous rocks are indeed quite common. In fact, they account for the vast majority of the upper layer of the earth's crust. And these igneous rocks serve a, um, useful purpose in that they can yield geologically valuable information on the make-up of the mantle and the conditions that existed there, in terms of heat and pressure.

Listening Practice 02

1. A 2. D 3. C

Listen to part of a lecture in a biology class.

Professor: And then, of course, there is the albatross. The albatross is an extremely large seabird... in fact, one type of albatross, the great albatross, is the largest flying bird in the world, with a wingspan of nearly 350 centimeters.

The albatross is renowned for its ability to, um... to travel great distances. Rather than a seasonal migration, however, the purpose of their journey is generally to seek out food. Albatrosses, you see, live on the open sea where food is plentiful, but when breeding season comes, they will nest in large colonies on remote islands, with each mating pair producing a single egg. When this egg hatches, the parents will take turns traveling for weeks to forage for food for their offspring, hunting for live fish and, um, other sea life, as well as scavenging for carrion. In fact, one individual albatross was tracked by researchers over a ninety-day period as it searched for food for its chick. They found that it flew nearly 25,000 miles in that time span... an astounding distance, equivalent to circumnavigating the entire earth.

Student: How can they fly so far? I mean, doesn't it burn a lot of energy and tire out their wings?

P: Well, first of all, albatrosses can store food in their digestive tracts, and they draw on this reserve of fat for energy when they need it. This also allows chicks to survive for weeks without sustenance while their parents forage.

But more importantly, when they fly, albatrosses use an energy-saving technique called dynamic soaring. What they do is use the force of the wind and the ocean's waves to their advantage, which allows them to glide for long distances without flapping their wings. Because of this, the only time they really burn energy during these journeys is when they take off or land. However, reliance on this technique has left them physically unable to flap their wings for extended periods of time, leaving them at the mercy of the weather. When confronted by calm seas and a lack of wind, a wandering albatross has little choice but to land and wait out the lull.

Listening Practice 03

p. 99

1. Ⓒ   2. Ⓐ   3. Primary - Ⓐ, Ⓓ / Secondary - Ⓒ / Surface - Ⓑ

Listen to part of a lecture in a geology class.

Professor: There are many things that move in waves, such as water, sound and light. But did you know that earthquakes move in waves, too? They do, and these waves are known as seismic waves. Today we're going to talk about the three distinct types of seismic waves produced by earthquakes. Now... um, all of these, all of these waves, they move through the layers of the Earth, sometimes bending or reflecting as they move from one layer to another. The first type is known as primary waves. These are the fastest-moving of the three, so they are the first ones we feel when an earthquake occurs. As they pass through the Earth's crust, they move at speeds of about five kilometers per second, which is nearly 20 times faster than the speed of sound. They can pass through solids, liquids, and gases, and when they do, the particles of the material are slightly pushed together and pulled apart.

Secondary waves, as you might guess from their name, are the next waves you're likely to feel in the event of an earthquake. They're generated at the same time as primary waves but move at half the speed. Unlike primary waves, they can't pass through gases and liquids—their movements are restricted to solid materials. And their effect on these materials is different as well. Rather than pushing and pulling particles, they shake them either up and down or side to side. Finally, we have surface waves, and again, their, um, their name gives you a clue as to their nature. They move through the surfaces of the Earth, in contrast to the other two wave varieties, which travel through its interior. Surface waves are the slowest and most destructive seismic waves, causing the ground to roll up and down. Studying these different types of seismic waves has been very valuable to scientists. Along with gaining a better understanding of the mechanics of earthquakes, they've also learned a lot about the characteristics of the Earth's interior.

iBT Practice 01

pp. 101-102

1. Ⓐ   2. Ⓑ   3. Ⓐ, Ⓓ   4. Ⓓ   5. Ⓒ   6. Ⓑ

Note-Taking

Every camera (film or digital) has lens, shutter, aperture
Right amount of light = shutter speed + aperture

Shutter speed
- time between a shutter opening and closing
- effect: motion & blur (slow shutter speed)
        frozen motion (fast shutter speed)

Aperture
- hole where light passes
- if aperture ↑ → shutter speed ↓
- effect: depth of field (the amount of picture in focus)
        larger aperture → small depth of field
        (blurred background, focus on main subject)

Listen to part of a lecture in a photography class.

Professor: Okay then. So, cameras... not as complicated as they may first appear. Essentially every camera, be it film or digital, operates in the same way. Think of your camera as a small box. This box contains a light-sensitive device that captures your image, or photograph if... if you prefer. There is also a lens through which the image can be magnified and focused. And then there's the shutter... through which light will travel onto your film or erm... digital sensor if that's what you use. Sequentially, light from your subject travels through the lens, through the hole in the box called an aperture, which I'll discuss in a while, and onto your film.

Now critical to any photograph is the amount of light available. Outdoors on a bright morning there is an abundance of natural light from the sun. But often we may take our pictures on a cloudy day or... indoors, meaning we have less light than on a sunny day or outdoors. Q6 🎧 To make the picture look right, we have to expose the film to the right amount of light. This is achieved through a balance of two factors: shutter speed and aperture. Fortunately, for those of us who aren't accomplished photographers, most cameras will adjust their settings automatically to ensure the right amount of light is used. If you leave your camera on auto mode, you'll hopefully get correctly exposed pictures all the time. **But to get really creative, you need to take control.**

Now, I just mentioned exposure, and this is where the shutter is important. It's best to think of the shutter as a window into the camera – the longer you leave the window open for, the greater the amount of light that hits the film, meaning a brighter image. You can choose how many fractions of a second you want, which um... means the time between a shutter opening and closing after you've pressed the shutter release. For instance, 1/30th, 1/60th, 1/125th, 1/250th of a second, and so on. Shutter speed has another interesting effect – motion and blur can be shown by slow shutter speeds, whereas motion can be "frozen" by fast shutter speeds. So, by err... selecting a shutter speed, you can give a creative edge to your photos.

Okay, the next thing we can influence is the camera's aperture. This is the hole through which the light passes in order to reach the sensor or film. The diameter of this hole can be controlled. So, for any given scene with a set amount of light, if you increase the aperture and double the amount of light entering the camera, the shutter speed will need to be put down by one stop, reducing the amount of light entering the camera by 50%. Also, the aperture changes the depth of field, which refers to the amount of the picture that will be in focus. In simple terms, the smaller the aperture setting is, the larger the depth of field will be. And by using a large aperture and thus having a small depth of field, the background of a picture can be blurred. This helps draw attention to the main subject of a photograph.

iBT Practice 02

pp. 103-104

1. Ⓑ 2. Ⓑ 3. Ⓒ 4. Ⓐ, Ⓓ 5. Ⓓ 6. Ⓐ

Note-Taking

Intro_ Desert animals & plants

1. Desert plants
   - to reduce water loss: small leaves covered in hairs or cuticle
   - long root to obtain water

2. Desert animals
   ① get water
     - from food
     - manufacture water metabolically (eg. kangaroo rats)
   ② avoid heat
     - cool down by panting, (birds) open beaks
     - hunt at night, sleep during the day

Listen to part of a lecture in a biology class.

Professor: The desert is a harsh environment with the hot sun beating down, no water, no shade... and Q5 🎧 although it might be an extraordinary experience to visit the desert, you probably wouldn't want to call it home. But to a myriad of animals and plants the desert is indeed home... and they're able to survive in this

most inhospitable place thanks to some remarkable evolutionary strides.

Q6 🎧 If you think about it, it's amazing that desert plants are able to exist in such dry conditions, growing in loose, sandy soil that provides so little nourishment. So, how do they do it? Well... plants generally lose a lot of water from the surface of their leaves through the process of transpiration. So... in order for desert plants to survive, they must find a way to counter this process. The leaves of these plants are usually comparatively small to reduce water loss and often covered in tiny hairs to provide protection from the sun, or by a cuticle, which is a, um, waxy coating that helps them retain water. Now, in order to obtain water, some desert plants make use of exceptionally long root systems... sending these roots deep into the earth and seeking out subterranean pockets of precious water. The roots of some desert trees will actually grow to lengths of up to 80 feet in order to reach life-sustaining supplies of water.

Animals, however, can't access water hidden deep underground, so they must find other means of quenching their thirst. Many have developed ways to get water into their systems without, um... without directly drinking it. Most can get some of the water they need from the food they eat, whether it's succulent vegetation, such as... cactuses, or the flesh of other animals. Some desert animals, however, don't have to get any water from their food sources. Kangaroo rats and some other desert rodents subsist on dry seeds and actually manufacture their water metabolically from the digestion of dry seeds. This metabolic water, incredible as it sounds, is all they need to survive. These highly specialized desert animals will not drink water even when it is given to them.

Now... along with thirst, heat is the desert's other great killer. To avoid excess elevation of body temperature, desert dwellers must find ways to allow the heat to dissipate from their bodies. Most animals can't sweat, but they can cool down by panting. Certain species of birds will open their beaks and vibrate their throats for a similar effect. Also, avoiding the intense heat of day is a priority, so many of these animals have adopted nocturnal lifestyles, you know... hunting at night and sleeping during the day. Others are crepuscular, meaning they hunt for food at dawn and dusk, when the sun isn't quite so strong. Either way, these animals spend the peak of the day safe in the shelter of cool underground burrows, thereby avoiding the worst of the desert heat.

iBT Practice 03

1. Ⓑ   2. Ⓓ   3. Ⓒ   4. Ⓓ   5. Ⓐ   6. Ⓑ

Note-Taking

Intro_ Egyptian calendar system

1. Major phenomenon
- Nile flooding? No, irregular
- appearance of Sirius (= beginning of year)

2. Lunar calendar
- based on the moon → shorter than a year
- very complex → second calendar

3. Civil calendar
- based on solar year, 3 seasons
- easy to manage
cf. why 3 seasons? river's cycle
    (Inundation, Emergence, Deficiency)

⇒ civil calendar for government
   lunar calendar for religious festivals

Listen to part of a lecture in a history class.

Professor: Class, we'll be talking more about Egyptian society today... uh, specifically, their calendar system.

Student 1: Was it like ours?

P: Well, there are similarities... but also some differences. First, Q5 🎧 can you guess what major phenomenon the Egyptians wanted their calendar to address? Remember, most people were farmers...

Student 2: Oh, the flooding of the Nile. Every year, the river would flood and then recede, leaving rich soil to plant crops in. Did they base a calendar on that?

P: **Um, you've identified the phenomenon, but the annual flooding of the Nile didn't occur on a regular enough schedule to base a calendar on.** But the Egyptians noticed another natural cycle... one that occurred at a regular yearly interval, and also coincided with the start of the Nile flooding. It was the appearance of a star, Sirius. They observed that the start of the flood usually closely followed the appearance of Sirius right before sunrise. So, they adopted this event as the beginning of their year.

S1: What about... did they divide the year into months like we do?

P: Well, yes... months were based on the cycle of the moon. Actually, that brings me to my next point. This early calendar was pretty complicated. Think about it. Each moon cycle is... about 29 days long. Twelve lunar months equal 354 days... 11 days shorter than the actual length of a year. But the Egyptians used a constant yearly event, the special appearance of Sirius, to mark the first day of each calendar year. This meant they had to employ a complicated system of rules to make sure the lunar months matched the appearance of Sirius every 365 days. Can you imagine trying to formulate a long-term schedule using this complex system?

Government administrators didn't want to. So, around 3,000 BCE, a second calendar was developed, one based closely on the solar year. It's known as the civil calendar... it's got three seasons, each with four months of 30 days. But that's just 360 days. To bring it up to 365, there were five special days added to the end of each year. The year still began with the appearance of Sirius, but now the months were more uniform and easy to manage.

S2: Um, Professor, you mentioned three seasons. Why not four like we have?

P: Good question. This goes back to where we started... the Nile. The Egyptians divided the river's cycle into three phases. There was Inundation, when the Nile overflowed; Emergence, when it receded and crops were planted; and Deficiency, a hot period of low river volume when the crops were harvested. There... the three seasons of the Egyptian calendar system. Q6 🎧 As a final thought, what do you think happened to the lunar-based calendar once the civil calendar was created?

S2: They probably just stopped using it, right?

S1: Because, yeah... why would you need two calendars?

P: Nope. Both calendars continued to be used. The civil calendar was for government, business... daily life... and the lunar calendar was for determining the dates of religious festivals. But both were interlinked by Sirius and the flooding of the Nile.

Vocabulary Review

A 1. recede   2. inhospitable   3. hinder
   4. nocturnal   5. formulate
B 1. Ⓑ   2. Ⓐ   3. Ⓒ   4. Ⓓ
C 1. Ⓒ   2. Ⓐ   3. Ⓓ   4. Ⓑ
D 1. out   2. that   3. mercy   4. out   5. thirst
E 1. Ⓐ   2. Ⓒ   3. Ⓓ   4. Ⓓ   5. Ⓐ
F 1. Ⓓ   2. Ⓓ   3. Ⓒ

UNIT 06 **Connecting Content**

Basic Drills   p. 113

1. Ⓔ – Ⓑ – Ⓒ – Ⓐ – Ⓓ 2. Aesthetes - Ⓐ,
Ⓓ / Victorians - Ⓑ, Ⓒ 3. Yes – Ⓐ, Ⓒ / No
– Ⓑ, Ⓓ

1.

Listen to part of a lecture in a biology class.

Professor: So how does a Venus flytrap eat a moving
insect? First of all, with sweet nectar the plant seduces
insects searching for food. When an insect lands on the
trap, it is likely to touch one of six, short... and stiff hairs
on the trap's surface. These are called trigger hairs, and
they serve as a primitive motion detector for the plant...
a bit like a tripwire. If an offending insect touches these
hairs enough to bend them, the leaves close down
upon it within half a second. The uh... the trap doesn't
actually close all of the way at first. Instead, it kind of
hesitates you know... it stays open for a few seconds
in order to allow very small insects to escape because
they simply... they wouldn't provide enough food. But
once the trap fully closes, the leaves form a strong seal.
The trap now serves as a miniature stomach. And just
like our stomachs, the trap secretes acidic digestive
juices. The insect is bathed in these juices over a period
of 5 to 12 days, during which the insect is digested and
nutrients are extracted.

2.

Listen to part of a lecture in a literature class.

Professor: "All art is quite useless." No, that's not my
personal opinion. That... that is a quotation from the
famous 19th-century British writer, Oscar Wilde. So
why, um, why did Wilde say that? For starters, you
have to understand that Wilde was an Aesthete—that
is to say, he was part of the Aesthetic movement. The
Aesthetes believed that the only purpose of art was to
enjoy it, an idea that was in stark contrast to the beliefs
of the Victorians of that era. The Victorians were strong
believers in the pursuit of higher education. They felt that
we should all be constantly striving to, er... to improve
ourselves, and that art should play an important role

to this end, teaching us moral and intellectual lessons.
Wilde and his contemporaries disagreed strongly.
Although they also valued art highly, they did so for
its pure beauty and the pleasure this beauty brought
them. So when Wilde proclaimed art useless, he was
not criticizing it. Rather, he was offering a new way of
approaching it.

3.

Listen to part of a lecture in a zoology class.

Professor: As you know, the Arctic is extremely cold, so
polar bears have had to adapt to survive in such a harsh
environment. One of the most essential mechanisms to
keep warm is in their fur. Polar bears' fur looks white,
but it is actually transparent so that most of the sun's
rays reach their skin. And their skin is totally black, so
it efficiently absorbs heat to keep them warm. Besides
absorbing heat, uhm... preventing heat loss is also an
essential strategy for polar bears. Their ears and tails
are so short that they don't lose any heat through them.
Actually, polar bears give off no detectable heat; they do
not even show up in infrared photographs. Polar bears
also have some special layers of fat, called "blubber,"
which help to protect, or rather uhm... insulate polar
bears from freezing air and cold water. And another
interesting thing is polar bears, unlike other bears,
don't er... don't sleep through the winter. Instead, they
undergo a state termed "walking hibernation" any time of
year when food supplies are scarce, in which their body
functions slow down to reduce energy wastage.

Dictation   p. 114

1. seduces insects searching for food 2. When
an insect lands on the trap 3. an offending insect
touches these hairs / within half a second 4. the
leaves form a strong seal 5. The insect is bathed
in these juices over a period of 5 to 12 days
6. he was part of the Aesthetic movement 7. the
only purpose of art was to enjoy it 8. art should
play an important role to this end 9. for its pure
beauty and the pleasure this beauty brought them
10. One of the most essential mechanisms 11. give
off no detectable heat / in infrared photographs
12. insulate polar bears from freezing air and cold
water 13. any time of year when food supplies are
scarce

Listening Practice 01

p. 115

1. C   2. Yes - A, C / No - B, D   3. C

Listen to a conversation between a student and a professor.

Student: Professor Walker? Can I ask you for some advice?

Professor: Of course, Darrel.

S: I plan on going overseas this summer as part of the college's study abroad program, but I can't decide on a destination. I'd like to go somewhere in Europe, but I'm not sure which country would be best.

P: I see. Well, there are certainly quite a few interesting countries in Europe.

S: I've been considering France. I studied French in high school, and Paris seems like a fantastic place.

P: Yes, Paris is wonderful. But it's the most popular destination for the program. Q3 🎧 There'll be a lot of competition, so the selection committee will be looking for a high grade point average. **Perhaps if you had studied harder...**

S: *[disappointed]* Oh, I didn't know that. *[brightening]* Well, what do you think about Scotland?

P: *[pause]* Scotland... hmm. Many of the students who go there seem to enjoy the experience, but I have to say... it's one of the program's least popular choices. Most students want to learn a second language while they're abroad, and that's not possible in Scotland, as they mostly speak English. I don't think it's a very appropriate choice.

S: *[disappointed]* Yeah... Is there anywhere else in Europe where they speak French?

P: They speak German and French in Switzerland. That gives you two useful languages to choose from. And academically, the universities in Switzerland are among the best in Europe. I've traveled there myself and really enjoyed my trip. I highly recommend it.

S: Wow, Switzerland... that's a good idea.

P: If you're interested, you'd better hurry. Switzerland is not as popular as France, but there are still plenty of students who want to go there.

S: I'll head down to the Student Center after my next class and fill out an application form.

P: Great. But don't forget, you also need to make an appointment to talk with a study abroad program coordinator. Until you do, they won't even look at your application.

S: Wow, I almost forgot about that. Thanks, Professor Walker.

P: You're welcome, Darrel.

Listening Practice 02

p. 117

1. B   2. C   3. Whistles - C / Clicks - A / Sound bursts - B

Listen to part of a lecture in a bioacoustics class.

Professor: When we think of sophisticated communication between animals, ocean-dwelling creatures might not immediately come to mind. But dolphins... dolphins are extremely intelligent creatures that use complex methods of vocal, um, interaction.

Now if you've ever been lucky enough to encounter dolphins in the wild, or perhaps at an aquarium, you know that they're constantly making some sort of noise... and these noises, they all serve specific purposes. The whistling sound you might hear them make, for example, is one of their primary forms of communicating. Each dolphin has a, um, a unique whistle which they develop at a young age. This is known as a signature whistle and it is used by dolphins as a means of identifying each other.

Then there are the clicking noises they make... short, sharp, high-frequency sounds produced in rapid succession. In fact, dolphins have excellent eyesight, but they rely heavily on the use of sounds because of the lack of visibility in their ocean environment. The clicking sounds allow dolphins to "see" in this situation. Well, this happens by... the clicks bounce off of objects in the distance, and the, ah, the time it takes for the echo to reach them, as well as the volume at which it arrives, gives the dolphins valuable information about what lays outside of their visibility. We call this echolocation, and it is especially helpful when dolphins are hunting, helping them to locate schools of fish in the distance.

Dolphins also make what we call "bursts" of sounds. These various groans, barks and other noises seem to signify how the dolphin is feeling. A, um, playful dolphin might squeak, while an aggressive dolphin would be prone to make more of a buzzing sound.

Well, this ability of dolphins to make vocal sounds provides us with fascinating research subjects. One of them is about whether or not the complex and varied means dolphins use to communicate constitute a language. While there are those who believe otherwise, based on experiments to date, it would seem that the sounds dolphins use aren't, um... well, they simply aren't structured enough to be considered an actual language.

Listening Practice 03

p. 119

1. Ⓓ   2. Ⓒ – Ⓐ – Ⓓ – Ⓑ   3. Ⓑ

Listen to part of a lecture in a meteorology class.

Professor: Another type of atmospheric storm is the tornado. Tornadoes are columns of swirling winds that descend from storm clouds until they make physical contact with the earth. They are generally funnel-shaped, with an average size of about 150 meters across. Tornadoes themselves are actually invisible – they are, after all, just wind – but water droplets and accumulated debris caught up in their vortex give rise to, um... to the familiar appearance we associate with these deadly storms.

Okay, well... tornadoes have a distinct life cycle like a living organism. First off, where do they develop? Well, tornadoes are spawned from supercell thunderstorms, which are storms that form from an updraft of warm, moist air that is tilted at an angle and rotating. This rotation occurs due to encounters with wind moving in different directions at different altitudes. The swirling mass that results is known as a mesocyclone.

Student: But Professor, isn't it true that not all tornadoes come from supercell storms... landspouts, for example, or dust devils.

P: Q3 🎧 I stand corrected. What I should have said is that most tornadoes are formed from supercells. There are exceptions, but they tend to be smaller, less destructive, and less common than the supercell variety.

Now, where was I? Ah, the birth of a tornado occurs when rain begins to fall from a supercell storm, creating a, um, downdraft of cool air which pulls the mesocyclone closer to the ground. At this point, a condensation funnel begins to shape, elongating until it reaches the ground. Once fully formed, the tornado continues to grow by feeding off warm, moist air, until it reaches a peak of size and speed. This is the mature stage, the point at which a tornado is at its most destructive. But eventually, the warm moist air is replaced by cooler, drier air, and as the tornado loses its source of energy, it enters what is known as the dissipating stage. It grows thinner, taking on a rope-like appearance, until it is blown away by surface winds and dissipates completely. At this point, we can extend the metaphor and say that the tornado has died.

iBT Practice 01

pp. 121-122

1. Ⓓ   2. Green form - Ⓒ, Ⓓ / Blue form - Ⓐ, Ⓑ   3. Ⓑ   4. Ⓒ   5. Ⓐ

Note-Taking

Problem: requested to paint 2 weeks ago, but no one showed up

Problem with the form?
- green for aesthetics, blue for necessities
  → filled out the right one
- checked a box: painters can't enter when she's out
  → painters visited twice, but...
⇒ Fill out a new form (faster)

Listen to a conversation between a student and a clerk in a student services center.

Student: Is this the Student Services Center?

Clerk: Yes, it is. How can I help you?

S: Hi, I put in a request to have my apartment painted two weeks ago but no one has shown up to do it.

C: Oh, let me see if I can find the form you filled out. What's your name?

S: My name is Alice Jacobs... and I was told at the time that the painters would show up within a few days. I thought maybe they are busy right now. Please check if I'm on the waiting list or something.

C: No, the painters aren't overly busy these days. They should have been in to paint your place immediately so I don't understand why you have been waiting two weeks. I'm thinking there must have been a problem with your form. What is your building and room number?

S: Oh, I'm in the Kennedy building in room 458.

C: Let's see here... and you filled out the green form, right? Not the blue one?

S: I think it was green, but I can't remember exactly. Why?

C: The green form is for cosmetic issues... you know... like painting or having carpet lain. The blue form is for necessities like if there is a problem with the plumbing or with the heating.

S: I think I filled out the right form, but if you can't find it maybe I did fill out the wrong form.

C: Give me a second... this office is such a mess. Aha... you said room 458 in the Kennedy building, right?

S: Right.

C: Well, you did fill out the right form. [slowed speech as if he is reading something] Perhaps the painters accidentally skipped over it... oh no... I see the problem.

S: What is it?

C: Look... you checked a box indicating that you don't want the painters to enter your place when you are not there. They left a note at the bottom of the form saying that they've been to your place twice but you weren't at home. You have to schedule a specific time if you don't want the painters to enter your apartment without you.

S: Oh! I'm sorry. I guess I wasn't thinking when I checked that box. I should have paid closer attention when I was filling out the form.

C: Q5 🎧 I can schedule a time for you if you like. Or, if you don't mind the painters coming by when you're out you can fill out a new form.

S: Which would be faster?

C: In general, it's faster if the painters are free to go into your place anytime.

S: **Okay, well, my parents are visiting this weekend, so I'd better do that.**

C: Okay, here's a fresh form for you. I'm sure the painters will get to it right away.

S: Thanks.

iBT Practice 02
pp. 123-124

1. Ⓓ 2. Ⓑ 3. Ⓒ 4. Yes - Ⓑ, Ⓒ, Ⓔ /
No - Ⓐ, Ⓓ 5. Ⓐ 6. Ⓒ

Note-Taking

Early settlements in America?
; Plymouth, Jamestown, and...

Popham
- lasted only a year
- King James gave the wealthy the lands

What made Popham fail?
1. Disease? medicine from England (X)
2. Winter? cold winter & no food (O)
          (Natives didn't help)
3. Lack of good leader: leaders died or went back

Failure was worthwhile
; contributed to rapid English expansion

Listen to part of a lecture in an American history class.

Professor: What place names come to mind when you think about early settlements on the east coast of America?

Student 1: Plymouth!

P: What else?

Student 2: Jamestown?

P: Yes, Jamestown was another. What else? *[pause]* Anybody? *[pause]* Hasn't anyone heard of Popham? *[pause]* No? Well, there's a reason for that... it didn't last very long. But when it was founded it was just as important to English expansion as Jamestown and later

Plymouth. See, even though the Spanish officially held title to all the New World, England wanted to establish a presence in that land. Q5 🎧 So King James gave some of his wealthiest subjects the right to claim land over in the New World, as they were the ones who could raise the funds. *[sarcastic]* **Who gave him the right to do that?** I don't know, but anyway... This group of landowners and aristocrats were collectively known as the Virginia Company.

S1: Aristocrats? I thought they were Pilgrims.

P: Ah... you're thinking of Plymouth... the Pilgrims founded Plymouth, but that wasn't until thirteen years later. Anyway, wealthy Englishmen came to the New World in 1607... some of them founded Jamestown, which was hugely successful and exists to this day. Popham, however, was abandoned after about a year. What made Popham fail while other settlements lasted longer? Any guesses what their problems were?

S1: Disease? Maybe they encountered new diseases they weren't used to.

P: Well, presumably yes, but the settlers arriving in Jamestown and later in Plymouth would have faced the same problem. Those settlements lasted, though. Actually, the early colonies with that problem were able to survive with medicines brought from England. So disease may not have been a critical problem at that time, I guess. Um, what else comes to mind?

S2: They probably weren't prepared for the winter.

P: Exactly, and they faced a bad winter... not what the Englishmen were used to. Popham was in a relatively northern part compared to colonies like Plymouth, so the colder winter made it harder to survive. Moreover, it was August when they arrived, which was too late to start farming. Contrary to Jamestown settlers who arrived in spring, Popham settlers lacked food, so half of them went back to England in December. Q6 🎧 There were a few troopers left hoping they could get help and resources from the Natives, but they couldn't. The Natives understandably didn't really trust the Englishmen because of their past experiences with them.

Another possible reason for Popham's decline was the lack of a good leader. The original leader died six months after their settlement and then his successor... well... his successor inherited a big estate back in England and left. By then the others gave up and went back with him. So that was the end of the Popham Colony.

So some people would say the colonists were victims of circumstances in a certain aspect, but umm... let me say their failure was somewhat worthwhile. The disappointed English backers of the Popham Colony learned valuable lessons about what was needed to survive in the New World. This experience later helped them found successful colonies. In this way, the struggles of the Popham colonists contributed to rapid English expansion.

iBT Practice 03

pp. 125-126

1. Ⓒ   2. Ⓓ   3. Judith Leyster - Ⓓ / Mary Beale - Ⓑ / Both - Ⓐ, Ⓒ   4. Ⓒ   5. Ⓓ
6. Ⓑ

Note-Taking

Intro_ Female artists
; from the Renaissance period

Female artists of Europe's Baroque era
1. Judith Leyster
   - no benefit from family (bankrupt) & supported herself
   - a member of guild & had 3 male apprentices
   - married another artist
   - well-known but only 2 works after her marriage

2. Mary Beale
   - 1st pro female English painter
   - parents: artists → good connections
   - painted portraits, breadwinner
   - husband assisted

Listen to part of a lecture in an art history class.

Professor: Okay... the history of women in the arts goes way, way back. However, it was not until the Renaissance period that a number of female artists gained international reputations. The propagation of new thoughts like humanism in this period maybe contributed to the status of women and appearance of female artists.

Uh, there's an awful lot we could say about female artists throughout history, so let me narrow the topic down. Q5 🎧 I'd like to focus on female artists of Europe's Baroque era, right after the Renaissance period. The Baroque era – it's not really important that you know much about it for the purpose of our lecture. **Suffice to say that the Baroque era began around 1600 in Rome and reached all of Europe.**

Now let me introduce Judith Leyster. She was born in 1609, in the Netherlands. The family she was born into wasn't, um, artistic. Her father was a brewery owner. So Leyster didn't have the benefit of a family-owned studio to get her started. She had to do it all on her own. On top of that, her father went bankrupt when she was fourteen years old, and she actually had to support herself with her paintings. A pretty tough thing to do, I'd imagine. But she was successful. How do we know? Well, she was mentioned by name as an active artist in a 1629

publication by Samuel Ampzing. She was a member of the Haarlem Guild of St. Luke... it was an artists' and painters' guild. She was one of just two women in the group. And – this is notable – she had three male apprentices. Leyster seems to have been influenced by the Dutch artist Frans Hals. Some say that she studied with him, but there aren't any records to show whether that was really the case. In 1636, she married Jan Miense Molenaer, another artist. She was well-known during her lifetime and esteemed by her contemporaries, but in a certain aspect, she was constrained by her role as mother. In fact, we only know of two works done by her after starting a family.

Student: Were there other professional female artists working during the same time period?

P: Yes, I was going to introduce Mary Beale. She was another artist of the Baroque period. She's been called the first professional female English painter. Her parents were both amateur painters, and Beale knew a lot of local artists... so she had some good connections. Beale made a living painting portraits... and seems to have been the breadwinner of her family. Her husband ended up losing his job. Actually, her husband worked as her assistant. He, um, mixed up paints for her and kept record books of her sittings.

S: *[impressed]* Really? Q6 🎧 Wow... she must have been pretty busy if she needed an assistant to keep track of her appointments. She must have made a lot of money.

P: *[supporting the student's statement]* **Well, in 1677 alone she had *[emphasized]* 83 commissions.** Okay... we're running out of time for today, but I'd like to continue our discussion of Mary Beale in tomorrow's class.

Vocabulary Review

pp. 128-129

A 1. extract   2. transparent   3. esteem
   4. metaphor   5. proclaim
B 1. Ⓑ   2. Ⓓ   3. Ⓒ
C 1. Ⓒ   2. Ⓐ   3. Ⓑ   4. Ⓓ   5. Ⓒ
D 1. succession   2. to   3. stand   4. date
   5. say
E 1. Ⓐ   2. Ⓒ   3. Ⓑ   4. Ⓓ   5. Ⓒ
F 1. Ⓒ   2. Ⓐ   3. Ⓓ

Inference

Basic Drills p. 133

1. (D) 2. (D) 3. (B)

1.

Listen to part of a lecture in an architecture class.

Professor: Contrary to popular belief, the Golden Gate Bridge over San Francisco Bay doesn't take its name from its distinctive orange color. The name is in fact a nickname invented by gold prospectors who entered the state via San Francisco Bay, and the bridge just uhm... just became synonymous with their quest for riches. Anyway, the color, called international orange, is quite astonishing for a bridge. So, how come the constructors selected this color? Well, because the bridge's paint must withstand harsh winds and salty weather, the engineers and architects tested various paints. Actually, there were three different colors that passed the test: carbon black, steel gray, and orange. While many people suggested the bridge should be painted in uhm... dull gray or black, architect Irving Morrow insisted on orange. And rightly so... it's because the azure Californian sky and deep blue waters contrast beautifully with the bridge suspended high above. It's also easy to notice for ships in the region that routinely battle against thick fog and driving rain. Ultimately, his idea turned out to be right, and now we can enjoy fabulous views of the orange bridge.

2.

Listen to part of a lecture in a zoology class.

Professor: Meerkats, you know those cute little furry critters from Africa, are well-known as altruistic animals since they're often seen doing guard duty while the... the others in their group forage for food in the ground. But this kind of behavior has been questioned by many scientists because it contradicts an animal's instinct for survival. Upon closer inspection, however, this role has distinct advantages over others. Now, if the meerkats' behavior was truly altruistic, the scientists reasoned, and I happen to agree, guards would be more likely to be attacked or killed. And also if meerkats guarded for others, they would not do guard duty when they live

alone. However, the scientists have found that none of these things actually happened. In fact, in the event of impending danger, the guard issues a series of short shrill cries before retreating underground more quickly than the other meerkats. In all reality, it is the safest role to occupy. Further research has revealed that meerkats stand guard when they have already eaten and probably have nothing else to do.

3.

Listen to part of a lecture in an environmental science class.

Professor: All around the world, bee populations are declining. Beekeepers have been raising the alarm about this for years. Now, however, it has been established as scientific fact that bee colonies are dying off. So we're finally looking at ways to take action. Although there doesn't seem to be a single cause, climate change is clearly a factor. Climate change affects nearly every form of life on Earth, but it hits bees particularly hard. This is because... how do I put this? They are less, um, adaptable than other species. As temperatures increase, you would think they'd migrate to cooler areas. But, generally, they don't. To make matters worse, climate change is affecting the blooming season of many flowers. This is another change bees must struggle to adapt to. So... why should we care about bees? Well, as pollinators, bees play a vital role in our ecosystem. If they were to suddenly disappear, so would some essential staples of the human diet, including certain fruits, nuts and vegetables. The bottom line is that we need the bees, so it is vital that we find a way to help their populations recover.

Dictation p. 134

1. doesn't take its name from its distinctive orange color 2. nickname invented by gold prospectors who entered the state via 3. must withstand harsh winds and salty weather 4. that routinely battle against thick fog and driving rain 5. it contradicts an animal's instinct for survival 6. guards would be more likely to be attacked or killed 7. they would not do guard duty when they live alone 8. Further research has revealed / probably have nothing else to do 9. as scientific fact that bee colonies are dying off 10. there doesn't seem to be a single cause 11. another change bees must struggle to adapt to 12. so would some essential staples of the human diet 13. so it is vital that we find a way to help their populations recover

Listening Practice 01

p. 135

1. Ⓓ 2. Ⓒ 3. Ⓑ

Listen to a conversation between a student and an employee in a college's student center.

Student: Excuse me, I want to get some information on arranging campus accommodation for my parents. Is it true that students can arrange for family members to stay on campus when they visit?

Employee: It sure is. You just have to present your student ID.

S: Okay, here it is. And... how long in advance do I need to book?

E: That depends. If there's a conference or a workshop being held, it is unlikely that you will get a room.

S: Is there anything planned for this weekend?

E: Unfortunately, there is. There's an environment conference going on on Friday, so all of the rooms are booked for Friday night. But Saturday won't be a problem.

S: Perfect! I'm performing in a jazz concert on Saturday night and my parents are coming in from Scottsdale to attend.

E: Oh, isn't that nice that they are coming all this way! So, I'll book a room for Saturday night. Is that correct?

S: Yes. So, what time can they check in exactly?

E: Anytime after eleven a.m.

S: Okay, thank you. Uh... well... *[hesitating]* I was thinking about taking them to Red River Falls. I don't have a car, though, and my parents are flying in. So, do you know of any other ways to get there? I'm sorry, I know you're not a travel agent and it's not your job to...

E: *[interrupting]* Oh, don't worry, we do this all the time. Red River Falls is a popular tourist destination so there's a shuttle bus going back and forth. I can write down the number for you. *[pause while she writes it down]* Here, you can call this number to find out the schedule.

S: Thanks. I appreciate it.

E: Q3 🎧 Oh, and by the way, Red River Falls can get pretty crowded. There's another waterfall nearby called Sunset Falls. It's not as well-known, but it's beautiful too. You can walk there from Red River Falls... it's only about a twenty-minute walk and the trail is well laid out with signs, so you won't get lost. You'll probably have it all to yourselves, and you can even go swimming.

S: That sounds great. **I will make sure that my parents take their swimsuits.** *[satisfied]* Thanks so much for all your help.

E: Anytime. Just let me know if there is anything else I can help you with.

Listening Practice 02

p. 137

1. Ⓒ 2. Ⓑ 3. Ⓓ

Listen to part of a lecture in a zoology class.

Professor: So, as we continue to discuss the various types of wildlife that inhabit the Rocky Mountain region of North America, I'd like to take a moment to talk about snowshoe hares. Well, they have to live in brutal North American winters alongside fierce predators, so they employ various strategies to survive such harsh conditions.

Firstly, their name is... as you probably know, derived from their large and furry back feet, which work much like a pair of snowshoes you or I might wear. They, um... they help the hares avoid their many predators by allowing them to travel quickly across deep snow without sinking beneath the surface. Besides, adult snowshoe hares can run at speeds of more than 25 miles per hour, making sharp turns and high leaps into the air in order to avoid pursuing predators, even jumping into water and swimming their way to safety, if necessary.

Young snowshoe hares, however, are not as fast. When approached by a predator, instead of fleeing, they will usually freeze and rely on the camouflage of their fur... because their fur, you see, is another important characteristic that aids their survival in winter. Twice a year, a snowshoe hare gradually sheds its coat of fur and grows a new one in its place. In the, um... in the summer, it's a brown color, but when the cold weather comes, long white hairs begin to grow, eventually becoming a new coat of white fur which allows them to blend in with the snowy landscapes of winter.

Another crucial issue during these long harsh winters is the availability of food. Most plants die in the winter, and those that survive are generally covered in snow. But snowshoe hares can survive on nutritionally poor diets because of the way their digestive systems are designed. Q3 🎧 Importantly, the gastrointestinal tract of snowshoe hares can handle all sorts of plant material, and they extract all of the available nutrients from their food by cycling it through their digestive system a second time. As a result, while other plant-eating animals might be at risk of starvation, snowshoe hares can subsist on plant stems, pine needles and tree bark.

Listening Practice 03   p. 139

1. (D)   2. (C)   3. (B)

Listen to part of a lecture in an art history class.

Professor: When we think about George Washington, the first president of the United States, a strong image generally comes to mind. Now, if you'll turn to page 154 in your textbooks, you'll see what I believe is the embodiment of that image... a photograph of a famous late 18th-century marble statue by the French sculptor Jean-Antoine Houdon. The subject, of course, is Mr. Washington.

This is a very popular statue, one that brings to mind images of democracy and American patriotism. But if you look over at page 155, you'll see another statue of Mr. Washington, created by Hugh Greenough in the 1830s. Although his physical portrayal of Washington is similar to Houdon's statue, to many Americans Greenough's statue doesn't seem like George Washington at all. So why does it have such a different effect?

Well, let's start with Houdon's statue. The style of the statue, along with the clothing Mr. Washington is wearing, was contemporary for the time. Mr. Washington is portrayed as a man, rather than a mythical figure, with a plow in the background and a walking stick in one hand. His other hand... what can you see?

Student: There're 13 rods. I think they represent the 13 colonies.

P: Excellent. Actually, these rods are an ancient Roman symbol of authority. There are 13 of them to represent the original 13 colonies, and they are mixed with arrows, a symbol of the American frontier. In essence, Houdon combined classical elements with contemporary ones, creating a style that Americans found appealing. Now let's move on to Greenough's statue. What is your opinion about it?

S: Umm... First, above all, it looks so awkward. He's wearing an ancient costume.

P: Yes, Greenough portrayed his subject in the classical style. Mr. Washington appears as the Greek god Zeus, shirtless and wearing an ancient robe. He sits in an unnatural pose, with one hand held to the sky. It immediately proved to be unpopular with critics and the public alike. This representation of Washington simply did not connect with most Americans, providing no relevance to their lives. Subsequently, it was moved several times, eventually ending up in a museum. Houdon's statue, however, remains where it was originally erected more than 200 years ago.

iBT Practice 01   pp. 141-142

1. (D)   2. (C)   3. (B)   4. (C)   5. (D)

Note-Taking

Problem: haven't received paycheck
       filled out necessary forms before deadline

→ School changed the main server and some TA's were deleted from DB
   Nobody knew who's deleted
   Fill out the form (originals were disposed of)

(angry) How long will it take? 1 week
    I have to pay tuition! I'll call and speed up the process

Listen to a conversation between a student and a university employee.

Student: Excuse me, I have a situation I was wondering if you could help me with.

Employee: What seems to be the trouble?

S: Well, I'm working as a teaching assistant, and I haven't yet received my paycheck. It was supposed to be in the mail two weeks ago, but I haven't received anything. The problem is I need that money now. Tuition is due this Friday and if I don't pay it on time, I will be charged a late fee.

E: Oh...

S: [interrupting] I don't know what the problem could be. I filled out all of the necessary forms a long time ago. And, of course, I got them in before the deadline.

E: I think I know what happened. You see, last month the school changed the main computer server. When that happened, a few of the teaching assistants were deleted from the database. You are probably one of those people.

S: [angrily] So they know about this? Why wasn't I notified when it happened? You said all this happened last month!

E: Because nobody knew about it until the paychecks went out and some people didn't get paid. A few TAs were in last week wondering where their checks were. Q5 🎧 We should have notified you sooner, but nobody knew who was deleted from the system. You know, there are so many TAs, it would be impossible to check. We just had to wait until they didn't get their checks and came to complain.

S: Okay, well I guess that's understandable. As long as it's ready now. **My name is**...

E: [interrupting] I'm afraid it's not ready. We didn't know who to make the checks out to. Now that we know who you are, we can prepare the check. All you have to do is

209

fill out this form.

S: But I already filled out this form. Why didn't they just check the forms? Did the TAs who came in last week have to do this?

E: Yes, I'm afraid they did. The original forms were disposed of after the information was entered into the computer.

S: This is ridiculous. *[pause]* How long is it going to be before I get paid?

E: Your check should be ready in a week.

S: *[angrily]* A week! But tuition is due this Friday! This whole situation is not my fault. I shouldn't have to wait a week for that money and then have to pay a late fee on my tuition. I can't wait a week.

E: I'm really sorry. I'll tell you what, I'll make a phone call to the accounting department and make sure they speed up the process. It's just one check and if they know tuition is due this Friday, they'll get it done for you.

S: *[grateful]* Okay, that sounds good. Listen, I'm sorry I got upset with you. I know none of this is your fault. I was just so frustrated. I really do appreciate all of your help.

E: No problem.

iBT Practice 02   pp. 143-144

1. Ⓓ   2. Ⓒ   3. Ⓑ   4. Ⓐ   5. Ⓒ   6. Ⓒ

Note-Taking

Intro_ What determines intelligence?

1. Neurons
   - neural network of central nervous system
   - exchange signals & send messages
   - shift in scrutiny to glial cells

2. Glial cells
   - assist activities of neurons (keep them healthy, functioning)
   - minor role? no
   - actively involved in synaptic communication

3. Relation to intelligence
   - Einstein's brain: smaller, but more glial cells than average ratio of glia to neuron ↑
   ⇒ but not proven

Listen to part of a lecture in a neurology class.

Professor: At one time or another, we've all heard the analogy equating the human brain to a computer. Any technicians could tell you what makes one computer more powerful than another, but what makes one brain more efficient than the next? What is it that determines our intelligence? Well... let's turn to the science of neurology.

Neurology focuses on the complex interconnected web of neurons that comprises the neural network of our central nervous system. These neurons are specialized cells that exchange signals by transmitting them across synapses... which are the, um, gaps between neurons that serve as the connecting medium for these exchanges. The neural network of an average person is made up of approximately one hundred billion individual neurons... all of them sending messages back and forth, dealing with the unfathomable volumes of information our brains process every day. These neurons are of fundamental importance. But lately there's been a... well, a shift in scientific scrutiny to something called glial cells as lots of essential roles of them have been discovered.

One hundred billion neurons... that's a mind-boggling number. But your neural network contains even more glial cells: more than ten times as many, in fact. These glial cells... or glia, as they are commonly known... provide vital assistance to the activities of neurons. Different types of glia serve different functions. All of them promote network stability by keeping neurons healthy and functioning. Some transport nutrition and oxygen to neurons, some recycle neurotransmitters emitted during synaptic transmissions, and, um, others... others hold neurons firmly in place with tiny filaments.

It was previously misconstrued that the primary function of glial cells was to serve as the structural support that held neural networks together. Scientists believed they played a very minor role in the transmission of signals, if any at all. We now know this is not true. Glia are actively involved in the process of synaptic communication... in fact, they are essential to it. Glia are the catalysts that initiate the development of synapses by neurons. As these synapses mature, glia maintain efficiency by regulating synapses as they take on specific roles within the neural network and eliminating any synaptic connections that are no longer needed.

So... how does this all relate to intelligence? Q5 🎧 Well, perhaps the greatest genius of modern times was Albert Einstein. When Einstein died, his brain was removed and examined. **Contrary to expectations, it wasn't found to be exceptionally large.** In fact, it was smaller than average. But when the number of neurons and glial cells in several different parts of his brain were counted, an illuminating fact was revealed. Q6 🎧 Einstein had 73% more glial cells than the average person... furthermore, his ratio of glia to neurons was quite high, leading some to suspect that this might have been the key to his brilliant mind. But, of course, this hasn't been indisputably proven. Today, as in the past, the workings of our brains remain somewhat of a mystery.

1. Ⓓ   2. Ⓑ   3. Ⓒ   4. Low-pitch – Ⓐ, Ⓒ, Ⓓ / High-pitch – Ⓑ   5. Ⓑ   6. Ⓒ

Note-Taking

Intro_ Elephants' communication

1. Infrasound
   - below the level of human hearing
   - how to know? feel vibrations
   - bigger animals → lower voices (like cello vs. violin)
   - travels farther without being absorbed

2. Use
   - call infants, send warning
   - find food
   - find mates
   cf. Only infrasound? high pitch sound when really scared

Listen to part of a lecture in a bioacoustics class.

Professor: For years, elephants puzzled many scientists and observers with their quiet communication. They appear to speak and listen to one another without making any audible sounds. But now we know they use a sort of secret sound to communicate. This special communication is based on infrasound. Umm, who can explain infrasound?

Student: Infra refers to something below and sound is sound. So, I guess infrasound is low-tone sound.

P: Good guess. Infrasound is sound below the level of human hearing. The frequency of a sound is measured in hertz, and humans can hear sounds at frequencies from about 20Hz to 20000Hz. The sound range of elephants is generally considered to be between 1 and 20Hz. The size of elephants...

S: [interrupting] Sorry, sir, but how can we know that such low-frequency sounds exist when we can't actually hear them?

P: Yes, you're right. We can't hear infrasound, but we can feel it. A certain level of low-frequency sound generates powerful ground vibrations. Q6 🎧 Scientists use special equipment like audiospectrographs to record and translate low-pitch sound waves into markings, and... **oh, I think I've digressed here. Where were we?** Umm... okay, the size of elephants. It's quite predictable that elephants make low-pitch sounds when we consider their size. Generally, bigger animals like whales and tigers have lower voices, just like a cello makes longer wavelengths and lower sounds than a violin. Well, the important thing is low-frequency sounds can travel farther without being absorbed or reflected by the environment. According to experiments, sounds of elephants are estimated to travel at least 4 kilometers. This long-traveling sound allows the six-ton animals to keep in touch across grasslands and forests in Africa and Asia.

The vast majority of infrasonic calling takes place in their daily lives. In breeding herds, mothers use low-frequency sounds when they call nearby infants. Elephant calves are prone to attacks by lions and hyenas. When a predator is spotted, older members of the herd send out warning calls so the rest of the herd can hear them and group together for protection.

In another situation like... umm, as you know, elephants live in groups, but they often scatter over large areas to seek food for their mighty appetites. In such circumstances, long-distance calls let elephants know where they can find food.

In addition, adult males and females also use infrasound to locate each other during mating season. Females, who only mate once every four years, make a special series of calls when they are ready to mate. The males who hear these calls rush toward the females.

S: Professor, I'd like to know if elephants only emit infrasound that we can't hear.

P: Good question. Let's see... the majority of elephant calls are rich in infrasound, but some include frequencies that humans can hear. For example, when elephants get really scared, like when they are threatened by lions, they let out very powerful, high-pitched calls.

Vocabulary Review   pp. 148-149

A 1. scrutiny   2. synonymous   3. neural
   4. patriotism   5. analogy
B 1. Ⓒ   2. Ⓑ   3. Ⓓ
C 1. Ⓒ   2. Ⓑ   3. Ⓑ   4. Ⓓ   5. Ⓓ
D 1. advance   2. out   3. dispose   4. derived
   5. take
E 1. Ⓓ   2. Ⓐ   3. Ⓓ   4. Ⓑ   5. Ⓒ
F 1. Ⓓ   2. Ⓑ   3. Ⓒ

Actual Practice Test

01
pp. 152-153

1. Ⓐ   2. Ⓓ   3. Ⓒ   4. Ⓑ   5. Ⓑ

Note-Taking

Purpose: job counseling

- Major? Biology
  (but interested in business, considering changing major
  → good, business-related work is easier to find)
- Skills? speak French fluently (+)
- Junior? sophomore (-)
- Work experience? no (-)

Options
① internship with pharmaceutical company
② internship with insurance company

⇒ Apply for both by next Friday
   Look over resume on Mon. afternoon

Listen to a conversation between a student and a professor.

Student: *[Knocking]* Can I come in?

Professor: Sure, have a seat.

S: I hear that you're the person to talk to for job counseling. So I'm here to get some advice about any jobs or internships that may be available.

P: All right. So what's your major?

S: I'm majoring in biology.

P: Okay, and I take it you'd prefer a biology-related job?

S: No, actually I'm more interested in business. I'm taking a management course that I quite like, and I'm considering changing my major. So I was kind of thinking if I got some work experience, it would help me make my decision.

P: That's a good idea. It will probably be easier to find business-related work, too. There isn't a lot of biology-related work in the private sector and there's not much you can do in academia or for the government until you've got at least a bachelor's degree. It's competitive, too. There are a lot of biology majors looking for work experience. It's a tough field. Anyway, do you have any special skills or interests?

S: Well... I can speak French fluently... my mother was from Quebec. So I'd kind of like to get involved in the field of international business in the future.

P: Good, bilingual and multilingual people are always in demand in a variety of fields. Let's see now... you're a

[hesitates, as if asking a question] junior?

S: No, I'm a sophomore.

P: Hmmm... that might be a problem. Companies usually hire people who are a bit older than a sophomore. Do you have any work experience to speak of? That might help.

S: No, not really.

P: Well, your French ability will go a long way. Let me think about what we can line up for you ... The first option that comes to mind would be to apply for an internship with a pharmaceutical company. Being a biology major will certainly help and it will give you experience that involves both your interests – science and business.

S: That sounds interesting. And... are there any other options?

P: The second option you might think about is to try to get an internship with an insurance company. I'm sure you've taken some statistics, right?

S: Yes.

P: Well, that will help you. And I don't think your age will be a problem because the company I'm thinking of hires about fifteen student interns every year. They offer a well-structured internship training program and you'll get a good idea of whether or not business is for you.

S: That sounds promising, too.

P: Tell you what... go ahead and apply for both. If you get accepted to both, you can make your decision then.

S: That's true. So, like, how do I go about applying?

P: **Q5** 🎧 You should apply by next Friday. Do you have a resume with you?

S: **No, not right now. Actually, it needs a few revisions.**

P: Okay, well, today is Friday, so you've got the weekend. I can... let's see... *[pauses to look at schedule]* I can look it over after my 8:00 seminar on Monday morning.

S: Oh... sorry... I have a class at 9:00 on Monday. Would Monday evening be okay?

P: Let me see... okay, that's fine. Just come by my office anytime after four and before seven.

S: Great, thanks a lot.

6. Ⓐ   7. Ⓑ   8. Ⓑ   9. Ⓓ   10. Ⓒ   11. Ⓑ

Note-Taking

Intro_ GMOs
1980 US Supreme Court decision
- allowed GMO patents

1. Led to many advances
- GMO bacterium producing insulin
- GMO crops
  → more nutritious
  → longer shelf life
  → easier to grow

2. Negative point of view
- Too many unknowns
- Long-term effects → on bodies? on environment?
- Want labels on food

3. Majority of scientists: GMO food is safe
- Help feed growing population

Listen to part of a lecture in an American history class.

Professor: GMOs... We all know what those are, right? They're genetically modified organisms, living things that have been artificially altered at a genetic level. There are many issues related to GMOs. Today I want to discuss one of the early legal issues. It centers around the following question: Can people and businesses legally patent the living organisms they create?

This question was, er, was presented to the United States Supreme Court way back in 1980. A scientist by the name of Ananda Chakrabarty worked for a large company called General Electric. **Q10** 🎧 He sought a patent for a genetically modified bacterium he had created. **And this wasn't just any old bacterium.** It was designed to consume and digest petroleum products. The idea was that it could be released into the ocean in areas where oil spills had occurred. Chakrabarty hoped it would provide a fast, safe and inexpensive clean-up method. It had the, um, potential to be a real money-maker for Chakrabarty. So he wanted to protect his creation. Ultimately, the court concluded that the fact that the bacterium was a living creature did not mean it couldn't be patented.

This was a huge decision. How you feel about it probably depends on how you feel about GMOs. On the one hand, the Supreme Court decision opened a door for researchers, inventors and businesses. **Q11** 🎧 Allowing them to obtain patents for their genetically modified organisms was very important. This is because the process of creating such organisms is difficult and expensive. If researchers felt they were unable to protect their valuable work from other companies... You know, companies that might copy their results... **Then they might not bother at all.**

But that's not what happened. The fact that their GMOs could be legally protected emboldened researchers to continue their work. This led to countless advances. Another GMO bacterium, for example, was created to produce human insulin for diabetes patients. There are also a number of crops that have been modified. In some cases, it was to make them more nutritious. In others, it was to give them a longer shelf life, or simply to make them easier to grow. Which leads us to the more negative point of view of the, um, of the Supreme Court decision.

When it comes to GMOs in our foods, the biggest problem is all of the unknowns. People are worried because we don't know the long-term effects they will have on our bodies and on our environment. It's a relatively new science, and there simply hasn't been enough testing. For this reason, many people are demanding more regulations on GMOs. For example, they want mandatory labeling of all food that contains genetically modified ingredients. The goal is, more or less, to slow down the flood of new GMO products that the 1980 Supreme Court ruling unleashed.

Personally, I can sympathize with the fears and concerns of these public health advocates. However, it must be noted that the majority of the scientific community believes genetically modified food to be safe. What's more, many see genetic modification as an essential tool in the race to find ways to feed our growing global population. Because of this, history may look back at that Supreme Court decision as an exceptionally wise one.

03

12. Ⓒ   13. Ⓓ   14. Ⓑ   15. Ⓑ, Ⓒ
16. Stratigraphic dating - Ⓓ / Seriation - Ⓑ /
Carbon-14 dating - Ⓐ, Ⓒ   17. Ⓒ

Note-Taking

Prehistoric art?
Art before written language (like Chauvet cave)

Dating method
1. Relative dating (by comparing)
   - can't get numerical age, but used for long
   ① Stratigraphic dating
      youngest layer at the top → compare strata
      but only minimum date
   ② Seriation
      track the stylistic changes
      but no linear development in art

2. Absolute dating (numerical age)
   - carbon-14 dating: measure amount of carbon-14
   - but age of material (maximum date) & the work must
     be scratched

Listen to part of a lecture in an archaeology class.

Professor: What is prehistoric art? Well, the word "prehistoric" refers to the period of time before written language. So… prehistoric art would probably refer to art produced by a culture during the time period before that culture had a written language. So, what's an example of prehistoric art?

Student: I believe the Chauvet Cave is.

P: You're right. It's a French cave with walls that are decorated with, um, prehistoric cave paintings. And can you tell me how we come up with estimates for the age of prehistoric art like the Chauvet Cave paintings?

S: I heard before that… there're dating methods… um, like carbon dating.

P: Good. You're right. Carbon-14 dating is one way that scientists determine the age of prehistoric art. Um, let's talk more about these dating methods. I'll get to carbon dating eventually, but first I wanna talk about something else. Relative dating. Relative dating is, um, a way of estimating the age of ancient artifacts. You… compare your ancient artifacts in a variety of ways… and that gives you clues about whether an artifact is older or younger than the things around it.

S: Well, then… is it a practical method? It sounds like it's not an accurate dating method.

P: Yes, you're right. Q17 🎧 You don't get an actual numerical age with relative dating, and you can only find out about an artifact's age relative to other artifacts or to

events. But, for a long time… um, archaeologists have used relative dating methods when trying to determine the age of ancient art.

Okay. There're two forms of relative dating I'm going to go over today. One form of relative dating is called stratigraphic dating. It relies on clues from the geological record to determine how old an artifact is. The geological record is divided into strata. You know that by "strata" I mean "layers," right? These layers of rock contain fossils and artifacts… and they form a kind of record of the past. The youngest layers are at the top. So, the older a layer is, the further it is from the top. In stratigraphic dating, you analyze the strata at one site, and then compare it to the strata of surrounding sites… and when you put it all together, you can develop a picture – a rough picture – of the relative ages of the strata… and the fossils or artifacts they contain. But, again, we only know the minimum date because the artwork may have been buried a long time after the work had first been made.

The other type I want to mention is, um, seriation. Instead of using geological clues to estimate an artifact's relative age, seriation uses stylistic clues. You know how artistic styles fade in and out of popularity? Well, archeologists look at artifacts and track the stylistic changes that occur over time. When they compare artifacts with different styles, they can get an idea about which is older… based on the style. But, the problem is there is no linear development in art. That's why we can't be sure which one is older than the other depending on the style. It's because a simple drawing doesn't always mean that the work is older than a complicatedly designed piece of art. Just like Picasso showed simpler designs than Michelangelo.

You mentioned carbon-14 dating. This is a form of absolute dating. Unlike relative dating, it can give a numerical age for certain artifacts. Organic artifacts. See, every living thing accumulates carbon. But when it dies, the amount of radioactive isotope carbon-14 begins to decay. Carbon-14 decays at a known, constant rate. So… we can measure the amount of carbon-14 in a sample and determine how much has decayed. Which tells us how much time's passed since the organism was, uh, alive. Technically, however, with this method we only know the age of the materials used in the artifacts, not the age of the work itself. So, we can determine the maximum date of the artwork. And… the work must be scratched in order to test it, so it could be damaged.

Actual Practice Test 2

01   pp. 160-161

1.   2.   3.   4.   5. Ⓓ

Note-Taking

a lab course

Q1 bring anything to the lab?
→ coat, goggles, notebook
→ timer: smartphone or stopwatch

Q2 grading
need only completing lab reports? → yes
→ grades mostly depend on tests

Q3 the reports help write professional papers? I aim for a career in academia
→ won't help you much
→ the first step to send yours to scientific journals

Listen to a conversation between a student and a lab instructor.

Student: Excuse me, Dr. Fernandez?

Lab instructor: Yes? Can I help you with something?

S: Well, I have a couple of questions about your lab course. Do you have a few minutes?

I: Sure. I'll do my best to help you out.

S: Great! This is my first time taking a college-level lab course, so I'm not sure exactly what to expect. I was wondering if we need to bring anything to the lab. In high school, they always provided us with all the equipment, but I heard it might be different here.

I: A little different, yes. There are a few things you need to purchase on your own. You'll have to get a lab coat, a pair of lab goggles, and a lab notebook.

S: Oh, okay. Do you know where I can get those?

I: You should be able to find everything you need at the school store. But make sure you only buy items specifically marked for laboratory work. There may be similar items available, but they won't be sufficient.

S: Okay. Is there anything else?

I: Well, make sure you have some sort of timer, so that you can keep track of time during your experiments. Most smartphones have that function, or you can bring in a stopwatch.

S: All right. My next question is about grading. Is it true that our only assignments are completing lab reports? There

won't be any worksheets to fill out?

I: Yes, other than performing the experiments, your only work for this class will involve writing lab reports. I think you'll find that's generally the way it's done at the college level. You won't get much busy work like worksheets. Your grades will most likely depend on one or two tests. Of course, that doesn't mean you'll have less work to do. It will just be more focused.

S: Got it. Okay, I just have one more question, and then I'll let you go. It's about the lab reports themselves. Are they designed to help us learn how to write professional research papers in the future? I'm aiming for a career in academia, so that would be really helpful.

I: Ah. So, about that. To be frank, I'm not a huge fan of the college's lab-report format, but my opinion on the matter doesn't seem to carry much weight. To give you a simple answer, the lab reports won't help you much in terms of writing full-blown articles for publication in science journals. They're just too simple for that. Mostly, they're designed to make sure that you understand the basic concepts of the experiments themselves.

S: Okay, I see. I guess that makes sense.

I: Don't be discouraged. The lab reports certainly aren't a waste of time. Think of them as the first step in a process. First, you learn how to write simple lab reports on prearranged experiments. Later, you learn how to write research summaries of your independent projects. Next comes your senior thesis, and after that you'll be ready to start sending your papers to well-known scientific journals.

S: I like the sound of that. Thanks for taking the time to answer my questions, Dr. Fernandez. You've been really helpful!

02   pp. 162-163

6. Ⓑ   7. Ⓓ   8.   9.   10.   11. Ⓓ

Note-Taking

Role of protein
- basic structural molecule
- cell repair, growth, maintenance

Millions of proteins are made of 20 amino acids
→ like alphabet, by rearranging their sequence
① body creates 11 amino acids (nonessential ~)
② 9 from our diet (essential ~)
  - animal products: complete protein (have all 9 acids)
  - plants: not all 9 → combine them

Listen to part of a lecture in a biology class.

Professor: Do you know what kind of role protein plays in the body? It's quite important because it, uh, it's the basic structural molecule for all the tissues in the body. It helps out with cell repair, growth, and overall maintenance. Protein makes up about, um, 17% of your total body weight. OK... let's take a closer look at protein. What's it made of? It's made of amino acids. They're like the... building blocks that form protein.

Q10 🎧 OK... the really neat thing about the way amino acid chains form proteins is this: all the proteins you find in living organisms – and there're millions of them – all of these proteins are made from just twenty amino acids. **That's right. Just twenty.** How do twenty amino acids create millions of proteins? Well... think of an alphabet. English, for example, has twenty-six letters that make up how many words? A lot... maybe 500,000... 600,000 words? This huge variety is made by rearranging the sequence of letters. The same is true for proteins. The properties of a protein will depend on the way the chain of amino acids is arranged. OK... but there's a major difference between the letters of the alphabet and amino acids. See, most words are made up of ten letters or less, but proteins... proteins can be made up of between fifty and 3,000 amino acids! Think of how many different sequences of amino acids you could have. If each of the amino acids is used once, there're approximately two quadrillion proteins that're possible. Anyway, I think I'm getting off track here. Let's get back to the amino acids in our bodies.

So, our bodies require twenty amino acids to perform those functions I told you about: growth... repair... maintenance... Our bodies have the ability to create eleven of these amino acids using other chemicals in our bodies. The eleven amino acids that we can make are called "nonessential" amino acids... and they're not essential to our diets. The nonessential amino acids are these ones: arginine, alanine, asparagine, aspartic acid, cysteine, glutamine, glutamic acid, glycine, proline, serine, and tyrosine.

All right. Q11 🎧 Twenty amino acids are required by our bodies, and we can make eleven of them. But what about the other nine? They have to be obtained through our diets. **You probably already inferred this, but they're known as essential amino acids** – they're essential to our diets. Here's the list of essential amino acids: histidine, isoleucine, leucine, lysine, methionine, phenylalanine, threonine, tryptophan, and valine.

Let's look at where amino acids in our diets come from. If you eat animal products like meat, milk, and eggs – those are mostly what we call "complete proteins," which refers to sources that contain all of the essential amino acids—those amino acids that we've got to get from our diets. Plant sources often don't have all of the essential amino acids. Rice, for example, is low in isoleucine and lysine. But different plant sources have different essential amino acids. Beans, for example, have an excess of lysine. By combining plant sources, you can get all the essential amino acids. So vegetarians, for example, can get all the essential amino acids they need by eating a variety of plant sources... say nuts, grains, and vegetables.

03   pp. 164-165

Note-Taking

Intro_ Market forms

1. Perfect competition
- conditions: atomistic, homogeneity, perfect & complete information, equal access, free entry
- hypothetical model

2. Monopolistic competition
- many sellers & consumers, free entry, information
- product differentiation (eg. Big Mac & Whopper)
- restaurants, books, clothing

3. Oligopoly
- a few, large sellers (influence each other)
- sellers work together: collusion
- barriers to entry
- cell phone service, steel, car

4. Pure monopoly
- 1 seller
- barriers to entry (because of patent or government's license)
- public utilities like gas, electricity…

Listen to part of a lecture in an economics class.

Professor: In economics, market structure, also known as market form, describes the state of a market with respect to competition. Today we're going to be discussing the major market forms – four of them.

Okay... first, perfect competition is one of the four economic models I just mentioned. Now, there's five, um... conditions that have to be met before you could have perfect competition. Q16 🎧 First, the market would have to be atomistic. **Well, what does that mean?** Think about the meaning of the word "atom." It refers to something small, right? Well, "atomistic" has that kind of meaning. In an atomistic market, there're a bunch of small-scale producers and consumers. Nobody's actions have much effect on anyone else's… 'cause they're such small parts of the market. The next condition – number two – is homogeneity. This means that all the products of all the different sellers are about the same. Homogenous. There is no product differentiation that could make consumers prefer a certain product. Third condition: perfect and complete information. This means that everyone – including consumers and sellers – knows the prices of all the other sellers. Fourth condition – equal access. All producers have access to the same technology and resources. The final condition is free entry… there are no obstacles for sellers entering or leaving the market. Therefore, anyone can be free to get into, conduct, and get out of business. So, that's perfect competition. In this model, no single seller makes abnormal profit. **Q17** 🎧 I wish I could give you some examples of perfect competition in the real world… but it's just a hypothetical model.

Now, let's look at a common market form that actually occurs in real life. Monopolistic competition. Like perfect competition, it has many sellers and consumers. And free entry. And sellers and consumers know everyone's price. The main difference is that sellers in a monopolistic market don't have identical products. There's "product differentiation." Like the Big Mac and the Whopper. They are basically similar products – burgers – but they have different characteristics. You know, there're differences in the ingredients, taste, packaging, as well as the price. So… the two sellers, McDonalds and Burger King, each market their burger to make it seem better than the other. In monopolistic markets, the purpose of product differentiation is to get an advantage over other sellers based on the features of products. Um, you can see monopolistic competition in markets for restaurants, books, and clothing, for example.

All right. Next is oligopoly. In an oligopoly, you have just a few sellers, which are generally quite large. They're all aware of what the other sellers are doing. Actions taken by one seller influence the other sellers, since there're so few of them. And since each seller has so much influence, it's beneficial for all the sellers in the oligopoly to work together, often to set prices. This is called collusion – when the sellers act together. In an oligopoly, there isn't the kind of free entry you saw in monopolistic and perfect competition. So that means there're a lot of obstacles for new sellers who want to enter the market. We call them "barriers to entry." Some examples of oligopolies are, um… cellular phone services, steel production, and car manufacturing.

The last model I'd like to mention is a pure monopoly. There're a couple of important characteristics of a pure monopoly. First, there's just one seller… so that seller has control over prices and there are no adequate substitutes for the product. Second, there're barriers to entry. Meaning, it's difficult for competitors to enter the market. Barriers to entry can be caused by things like, um, one company holding the patent for a certain product, or one seller being licensed by the government to be a monopoly. Some examples of monopolies include public utilities, like gas, electricity, water… um, and local telephone companies.

Actual Practice Test 3

01

pp. 168-169

1. C   2. D   3. B   4. C   5. A

Note-Taking

Purpose: ask about research paper

Observe a child's behavior and report it?
- No! ① observe without interaction
     ② make predictions (check the literature)
     ③ observe again & see if predictions are right
- Grade is based on how you interpret
- Final report includes: outline, description, sources,
   analysis, prediction...
- Example (my daughter)
using imagination = preoperational stage
→ next step: thinking abstractly, rationally

⇒ Go to the education department to schedule time and
   subject

Listen to a conversation between a student and a professor.

Student: *[knocking]* Can I come in?

Professor: Sure, have a seat, Brian.

S: Thanks. Q5 🎧 So... I missed class on Thursday because I wasn't feeling well and I heard that we have a research paper due in May. But... well... it sounds kind of simple, so I wanted to make sure I wasn't missing anything. All we have to do is observe a child's behavior and report it? That seems kind of...

P: *[interrupting]* **Oh, that's not all, Brian, that's only the beginning.** Who told you that was all you have to do? Have them see me because the project is a bit more complicated than that.

S: Er... okay... I'll tell her. So... what else do we have to do?

P: Well, as you know, the first step in the project is observe a child for about twenty minutes. Now, when I say observe, I mean just that. You don't interact with the child in any way, so he or she will behave naturally.

S: Okay, but I don't understand what I'm supposed to be researching. What are we testing for? I mean... what are the variables?

P: There are none. It's an observational study, which allows you to make predictions based on what you observe and what you learn through your study. As you know, children behave differently depending on what stage of their development they are in. You will first observe the child and then check the literature to determine what stage of development the child is in. Then, you can make predictions about the child's behavior.

S: I see... so... do I get to do a follow-up?

P: Yes, that's the final step in the project. In a few months you will observe the child's behavior again and see if your predictions are realized.

S: So... is our grade based on whether or not we confirm our hypothesis?

P: No, no... absolutely not. The point is to learn something. Your grade will be based on how you interpret the results. What does it mean? What does it suggest? What further predictions can you make?

S: So, what should be included in the final report?

P: First, you outline the whole procedure, and then describe your initial observations. These should be as objective as possible... just describe what you saw without any speculation. Then refer to the literature... be sure to cite your sources... to do your analysis and make your predictions. Then, once again, you should describe the second observation. Finally, do your analysis and make further predictions.

S: *[unsure]* Uh... okay...

P: Why don't I give you an example. My four-year-old daughter can sit in an empty room and entertain herself by creating an imaginary situation. The other day, she was playing as if she were at the seashore even though there was no sand or water. What does that tell you?

S: Well, she's not crying for her parents, so she's becoming independent. She's also using her imagination.

P: Good. You've brought up imagination; that's the preoperational stage according to Piaget's cognitive stages. So what prediction can you make from that?

S: Well, the next step is... I guess she'll be ready to think abstractly. And she will be able to make rational judgments soon.

P: Excellent. Do you think you understand now?

S: Yes.

P: Great, now you need a child to observe. What you can do is go to the Education Department. There is an assistant named Mr. Kelly who can help you. He has a list of parents who take part in our developmental psychology projects by volunteering to have their children observed. Mr. Kelly can schedule a time and a subject for you. I advise you make the appointment as soon as possible because there has to be a three-month interval between observations.

S: *[enthusiastic]* Right... I'll get right on it. Thanks.

6. Ⓐ   7. Ⓓ   8. Ⓑ   9. Ⓑ   10. Ⓒ   11. Ⓓ

Note-Taking

Intro_ Big size prehistoric insect fossils

1. How or why so big?
- the amount of oxygen then: 35% (now 21%)

2. oxygen content vs. insect's size
- insects have different respiratory system: tracheae
- oxygen concentration ↑ → travels further → bigger insect
  (still a theory)
- evidence: research
  → small bugs: less affected by oxygen amount
  → big bugs: stop hopping in low oxygen

Listen to part of a lecture in a paleobiology class.

Professor: Imagine that you're standing in line at the grocery store, waiting to check out. The tabloids are displayed on a rack nearby, so you start reading the headlines. You see stuff like this: DOG-SIZED COCKROACH BITES DELIVERY PERSON! ARMY OF MAN-EATING ANTS INVADES VANCOUVER! Sure, these headlines may sound far-fetched… but new research suggests that they might not be completely fictional. What do I mean? Well, scientists have found fossils of a prehistoric dragonfly that lived about 250 million years ago during, uh, what we call the Paleozoic Era. And their size… they had a full wingspan of 30 inches and a body length of 18 inches.

Now I'm sure the question on everyone's mind is, well, in the past, how or why could insects get so big? The answer, um, might have to do with the amount of oxygen present then. **Q11** 🎧 Nowadays, there's about, how much, um, 21 percent oxygen in the atmosphere, right? Well, back during the Paleozoic Era, the oxygen content was as high as 35 percent. It may have been that around 400 million years ago the recently evolved oxygen-producing plants on Earth contributed to the, um, change in the oxygen content. **Um, but that's not really what we're talking about today.** We're going to be talking about these huge insects… and how the amount of oxygen present in the Paleozoic Era is related to their size.

So, scientists believe that the amount of oxygen in the atmosphere might have made it possible for insects to grow bigger than they can now. So… how would oxygen limit or increase maximum size? Well, it all has to do with the way insects breathe; their respiratory systems. As you know, insects don't have lungs. They actually have a different setup. Um, it's a system of tubes known as tracheae. Air comes into the tubes through holes on the insect's abdomen, and then it flows down the tubes. Now, the key here is that the distance oxygen can travel down the tubes is determined by the concentration of oxygen in the air. That means, the higher the oxygen concentration, the further it can travel through the tubes. So… the higher the oxygen concentration, the longer the tracheae can be… and the bigger an insect can become.

Um, this idea about insects' size being a result of oxygen concentration is still a theory… and scientists aren't positive about it… but there is some evidence for it. Um, Jon Harrison, a professor and researcher at Arizona State University, has conducted research on modern-day insects to figure out what effect oxygen concentration in air has on their activities. The results were pretty much what he expected – smaller insects were less affected by a decrease in the amount of oxygen in the air. He found that small grasshoppers can hop continuously in an environment where the oxygen concentration is lower than the normal concentration in air. The very smallest grasshoppers could even keep hopping when the concentration of oxygen was just 5 percent. Of course, the bigger grasshoppers wore out faster and would stop hopping altogether. But, when Harrison put them in an environment with more oxygen… like a concentration of 40 percent… um, in that case the large grasshoppers would hop more. The same results were true when Harrison tested the ability of dragonflies to fly in low- or high-oxygen environments. And again, we don't know what exactly happened 300 million years ago, but I think Harrison's findings are reliable evidence to support the theory.

| 12. C | 13. B | 14. D | 15. B | 16. A |
| 17. D |

Note-Taking

What's a spectrum? (pl. spectra)
- different colors of light
- rainbows: visible spectrum (or optical spectrum)
        part of electromagnetic spectrum
                → made up of radiation of all different
                    wavelengths

Radiation is dangerous? process of emitting energy
(neutral)

Use of spectra
- astronomers break up light from star
- absorption lines: dark lines where specific wavelengths
                were absorbed
                    unique to each atom
    → what the star is made of, what gases are
        eg. sunlight: discovery of helium

Listen to part of a lecture in an astronomy class.

Professor: Okay, um, so today we're gonna talk about spectra. Of course, that's the plural term for the Latin word "spectrum." Q16 🎧 What's a spectrum? It's the different colors of light that a star gives off. Although it may look like a single color of light, it's actually made up of different colors. **Chances are, you've seen a spectrum with your own eyes. Ever seen a prism turn sunlight into rainbows?**

Let's talk for a minute about the rainbow of colors you see when sunlight passes through a prism. Red, orange, yellow, green, blue, indigo, violet. Together, these are what we call the visible spectrum – or the optical spectrum. The visible spectrum's just one part of what's called the electromagnetic spectrum. You might already know, but the electromagnetic spectrum is made up of radiation of all different wavelengths. On one end there're gamma rays, and on the other end are radio waves. And in the middle there's UV radiation, infrared radiation, and the visible spectrum, among other things. So, visible light is electromagnetic radiation that's visible to the human eye.

Student: Q17 🎧 Excuse me, professor? The electromagnetic radiation you're talking about... is it dangerous?

P: You mean because it's "radiation."

S: Right. Radiation causes cancer, doesn't it?

P: Well, the term "radiation" refers to the process of emitting energy. It's pretty much just energy moving through space. It's a neutral term. **But... to the general public, the word "radiation" is used to mean "ionizing radiation."** That's the kind of radiation that's damaging to cells. And we're just going to use the term in its broad meaning in this class, okay? Now let's get back to spectra. Specifically, to the spectra we see from stars.

Um, the spectra that come from stars are useful to astronomers. See, when they break the light from stars into separate colors – and they do this in a way that's similar to the way a prism turns sunlight into rainbows – anyway, when astronomers break up the light from a star, they can get key information from it.

How does this work? Well, in a star, radiation passes from the center of the star out toward the lower-density gases in the upper layers of the star. When radiation passes through low-density gases, something interesting happens. Atoms of the star's gases can absorb certain wavelengths... or colors. This happens basically for atoms to get energy from the passing radiation.

So what does that do for the star's spectrum? Well, if you look at a spectrum... a rainbow, you'll see these dark lines where the specific wavelengths were absorbed. Those are called absorption lines. Each atom has its own set of absorption lines like a fingerprint. Take hydrogen, for example. Hydrogen atoms absorb specific wavelengths of violet, cyan, and red. So in that spectrum, there'd be gaps... absorption lines... in the violet, cyan, and red. Get it? Anyway, since the absorption lines are unique to each atom, it's possible to figure out what gases are present by looking at a spectrum.

So astronomers can look at the absorption lines in the spectrum of a star and actually figure out what the star is made of... what gases are in the star. All of this is based on the absorption lines in the spectrum.

In fact, the spectrum of our very own star – the Sun – led to the discovery of helium. It's a pretty important discovery, um, considering that helium is the second-most-abundant element in the universe. It was discovered independently by two astronomers in the same year. The French astronomer Pierre Janssen and the English astronomer Joseph Norman Lockyer both observed helium in the spectrum of the Sun in 1868. The spectrum they saw didn't match up with any of the known elements at the time. Eventually, it was named helium... for the Greek word helios, meaning "sun." So, as you can see, the spectra of stars have a lot to tell us.